Buffy the Vampire Slayer™

The Script Book

Season Two, Volume Four

"Killed by Death"	1
"I Only Have Eyes For You"	57
"Go Fish"	114
"Becoming, Part One"	168
"Becoming, Part Two"	226

Pocket Books

New York   London   Toronto   Sydney   Singapore

Historian's Note: These teleplays represent the original shooting scripts for each episode; thus we have preserved any typos and misattributions. The scripts may include dialogue or even full scenes that were not in the final broadcast version of the show because they were cut due to length. Also, there may be elements in the broadcast that were added at a later date.

This book is a work of fiction. Any references to historical events, real people, or real locales are used fictitiously. Other names, characters, places, and incidents are the product of the author's imagination, and any resemblance to actual events or locales or persons, living or dead, is entirely coincidental.

First Pocket Books edition March 2003

™ and © 2003 by Twentieth Century Fox Film Corporation. All Rights Reserved.

POCKET BOOKS
An imprint of Simon & Schuster
Africa House
64-78 Kingsway
London WC2B 6AH

All rights reserved, including the right of reproduction in whole or in part in any form.

Printed in the United States of America
10 9 8 7 6 5 4 3 2 1

A CIP catalogue record for this book is available from the British Library

ISBN 0-7434-6777-9

Episode # 5V18
Story # 4765

BUFFY THE VAMPIRE SLAYER

"Killed By Death"

Written By

Rob DesHotel

&

Dean Batali

Directed By

Deran Sarafian

SHOOTING SCRIPT

February 2, 1998 (WHITE)

BUFFY THE VAMPIRE SLAYER

"Killed By Death"

CAST LIST

```
BUFFY SUMMERS.......................... Sarah Michelle Gellar
XANDER HARRIS.......................... Nicholas Brendon
RUPERT GILES........................... Anthony S. Head
WILLOW ROSENBERG....................... Alyson Hannigan
CORDELIA CHASE......................... Charisma Carpenter
ANGEL.................................. David Boreanaz

JOYCE SUMMERS.......................... Kristine Sutherland
DR. WILKINSON..........................*Juanita Jennings
DR. BACKER............................. Richard Herd
DON.................................... Willie Garson
RYAN...................................*Andrew Ducote
CELIA..................................*Denise Johnson
LITTLE BUFFY...........................*Mimi Paley
INTERN.................................*Robert Munic
*KINDESTOD.............................*James Jude Courtney
```

BUFFY THE VAMPIRE SLAYER

"Killed By Death"

SET LIST

INTERIORS

SUNNYDALE HOSPITAL
    ENTRANCE AREA
    WAITING AREA
    CORRIDOR
    ANOTHER CORRIDOR
    BUFFY'S ROOM
    KIDS' WARD
    RECORDS ROOM
    DR. BACKER'S OFFICE
    BASEMENT
    STAIRWELL

SUNNYDALE HIGH SCHOOL
    LIBRARY

DIFFERENT HOSPITAL
    HOSPITAL ROOM

BEDROOM

BUFFY'S BEDROOM

EXTERIORS

CEMETERY

SUNNYDALE HOSPITAL
    COURTYARD

BUFFY THE VAMPIRE SLAYER

"Killed By Death"

TEASER

1   EXT. CEMETERY - NIGHT   1

Another CREEPY NIGHT among the tombstones.

We PAN along the cemetery wall and TILT UP. A HAND comes over the top. A beat. Then ANOTHER HAND comes over. BUFFY hoists herself into view. She rests for a moment. Her face is pale, her eyes sunken, her hair mussed up -- not the bright and shiny Buffy we're accustomed to seeing.

Buffy wearily SWINGS her leg over the wall. With great effort, she PULLS the rest of her body over, then DROPS to the ground, STUMBLING a bit. She puts a hand against the wall and steadies herself, feeling DIZZY.

                    BUFFY
           Whoa...

She pulls a stake from her bag and begins to MOVE along the wall, scoping out the place.

She HEARS someone near the gate and PRESSES herself against the wall, inching towards the sound. She lifts her stake, STEPS around the corner, and nearly PLUNGES her stake into--

                    XANDER
           DYEAAH!

--who JUMPS away, startled.

                    BUFFY
           Non-vampire.

Buffy sees WILLOW and CORDELIA behind him.

                    BUFFY (cont'd)
           Plus two.

                    WILLOW
               (meekly)
           Hi.

                                                          CONTINUED

1 CONTINUED: 1

                 XANDER
              (composing himself)
      Man, Buffy. My whole life just
      flashed before my eyes.
              (then)
      I've got to get me a life.

Buffy puts the stake back in her belt.

                 BUFFY
      What are <u>you</u> doing here?

                 WILLOW
      What are you doing here?

                 BUFFY
      Patrolling.

                 WILLOW
      Buffy, you're sick.

                 BUFFY
      I feel fine. The ground's moving
      around a little bit, but I like it.
      It's like a ride.

                 CORDELIA
      Half the school is out with this flu,
      Buffy. It's a serious deal. We're
      all worried about how gross you look.

                 BUFFY
      I'm touched. I have work to do.

                 WILLOW
      Come on, Buffy. One night of rest
      isn't going to kill you.

                 BUFFY
      But it might kill someone else.

                 XANDER
      You mean Angel might.

Buffy looks at them for a moment, then:

                 BUFFY
      You guys should go find a safer place
      to be. Like somewhere I'm not.

                                            CONTINUED

1 CONTINUED: (2)   1

                    XANDER
          Buffy, this isn't the time to
          challenge Angel for the Ultimate
          Fighting Championship. He's at full
          strength, and you're only half a
          slayer.

                    BUFFY
          But I'm still the Slayer. And as
          long as I am, Angel's not going to
          kill anyone else.

From behind her, she hears:

                    ANGEL (O.S.)
          Oh, come on. Just one more.

Buffy turns to see ANGEL. All vamped out.

He LUNGES at the trio. They SCATTER, but Angel DIVES and grabs Cordelia, who FALLS to the ground, screaming.

Buffy GRABS Angel and LIFTS him to face her (as Cordelia SCAMPERS away). Buffy has a stake in her right hand, raised and ready to plunge.

She starts to bring the stake down. Angel CATCHES her wrist and BENDS her hand backwards--

                    BUFFY
                 (pained)
          Ahh!

--until she drops the stake.

                    ANGEL
          Not feeling well, lover?

Buffy surprises him with a LEFT HOOK out of nowhere. He reels a bit.

                    BUFFY
          That helps.

Angel RAMS his shoulder into her chest and SLAMS her against   *
a gravestone, knocking the wind out of her.

BUFFY'S POV: is blurry.

She sluggishly tries to hold Angel off, but he staggers her with a series of HITS and KICKS.

                                                        CONTINUED

1 CONTINUED: (3) 1

Buffy stumbles away and tries to focus on Angel. She SWINGS at him a few times, misses.

An amused Angel watches her struggle.

              ANGEL
    You know, you being off your game?
    It's kind of taking all the fun out
    of this.

He smashes his FIST into her face.

              ANGEL (cont'd)
    Nope. Still fun.

He JUMPS on her and they ROLL on the ground until he is on top of her.

              ANGEL (cont'd)
    Uh-oh. This does not look good for
    our heroine.

Suddenly, Buffy's weapons bag is PULLED over Angel's head, blinding him.

REVEAL: Willow standing behind him, holding the bag on.

Xander sends a couple of PUNCHES to Angel's torso. Angel ROLLS off of Buffy, RIPS the bag off his head and turns to face Willow, Xander and Cordelia.

They stand there between him and Buffy, each holding a cross.

              ANGEL (cont'd)
    We'll have to do this again some time.

Angel TURNS and HEADS OFF.

Buffy struggles to her feet; puts her hand to her head.

              BUFFY
    I told you guys to leave.
        (a beat)
    This is my fight. You don't have
    to...

Her eyes ROLL BACK in her head and she COLLAPSES. Xander quickly moves down to her.

              XANDER
    Buffy, are you all right?

CONTINUED

1   CONTINUED: (4)   1

   She doesn't respond. He takes her by the shoulders.

                    XANDER (cont'd)
              Buffy?

CLOSE ON:

   Buffy's lifeless body.

                                        BLACK OUT.

                    END OF TEASER

BUFFY THE VAMPIRE SLAYER "Killed By Death" (WHITE) 2/2/98   6.

ACT ONE

2   INT. SUNNYDALE HOSPITAL ENTRANCE AREA - LATER THAT NIGHT   2

A cold, antiseptic, dreary place. Eerily silent. PATIENTS in various states of illness and injury sit waiting.

The calm is shattered as Xander BURSTS through the hospital doors, carrying Buffy. Willow and Cordelia run alongside.

>   XANDER
> We need help!

>   WILLOW
> Somebody, please! Now!

A few HOSPITAL STAFF MEMBERS rush to them.

>   INTERN
> What happened?

| XANDER | WILLOW | CORDELIA |
| She fell. | The flu. | She fainted. |

>   XANDER (cont'd)
> The flu, fainted and fell. She's
> <u>sick</u>! Make it better!

Buffy is placed on a gurney and WHEELED down the hall as the INTERN begins to examine her. Buffy's friends crowd around.

>   INTERN
> The patient is unconscious.
>   (examining eyes)
> Pupils are unequal and unresponsive.

>   CORDELIA
> What does that mean?

>   WILLOW
> Is she going to be okay?

>   INTERN
> People, you need to give us some
> room, here!

Still on the move, they meet up with another doctor, a woman in her mid-thirties. This is DR. WILKINSON.

>   DR. WILKINSON
> What've we got?

CONTINUED

2   CONTINUED: 2

                    INTERN
          Teenage girl, high-grade fever,
          possible fractures.

                    DR. WILKINSON
          Get her into Trauma One. Give me a
          CBC, chem 7, type and screen.

They wheel her into a room. Xander and the girls start to
follow them in. Dr. Wilkinson stops them.

                    DR. WILKINSON (cont'd)
          Excuse me, you're going to have to
          wait out here.

                    XANDER
          Someone should be with her.

                    DR. WILKINSON
          You're going to have to wait out here.

Dr. Wilkinson hurries inside, swinging the door closed.
Willow turns to Xander.

                    WILLOW
          I'll call Giles. Tell him what
          happened.
               (then, to Cordelia)
          Call Buffy's mom. Tell her... not
          what happened. Just get her here.

The girls go off as Xander looks through a window, into the
emergency room.

                    XANDER
               (trying to believe it)
          She's going to be okay.

XANDER'S POV through the window:

as the Slayer lies near death. Doctors and nurses surround
her in a flurry of activity.

                                        DISSOLVE TO:

3   INT. SUNNYDALE HOSPITAL WAITING AREA - LATER (NIGHT)   3

GILES is there with Xander, Willow, and Cordelia as JOYCE
comes rushing in.

                                                       CONTINUED

3 CONTINUED: 3

                    JOYCE
        Where is she?

                    GILES
        Still in the emergency room.

                    JOYCE
        I want to see her.

                    CORDELIA
        They won't let us in.

Dr. Wilkinson comes over.

                    DR. WILKINSON
        Ms. Summers? I'm Dr. Wilkinson.

                    JOYCE
        Is Buffy okay?

                    DR. WILKINSON
        We were able to stabilize--

                    JOYCE
        Is she _okay_?

                    DR. WILKINSON
        She's going to be fine.

Joyce lets out a breath.

                    JOYCE
        Thank you.

                    XANDER
        Good. Good. That's good.

                    DR. WILKINSON
        I want to keep her here a few days,
        though. She's still got some healing
        to do.

                    GILES
        Was she hurt badly?

                    DR. WILKINSON
        The injuries from the fall were
        minor: Sprained wrist and a couple of
        cracked ribs. I'm more concerned
        about her fever.

                                                        CONTINUED

3 CONTINUED: (2) 3

>   JOYCE
>   She said this morning she was feeling
>   better.
>
>   DR. WILKINSON
>   She will be. But she's still
>   suffering from exhaustion and
>   dehydration.
>
>   WILLOW
>   I keep telling her that Yoo-Hoo is
>   not a fluid replenisher.
>
>   DR. WILKINSON
>   Come on. I'm sure you want to see
>   her.

4 INT. SUNNYDALE HOSPITAL CORRIDOR - A MOMENT LATER (NIGHT) 4

Buffy is wheeled on a gurney out of the ER and into the
hallway, where Joyce and the others wait. Her sprained wrist
(from the Angel encounter) is wrapped with a bandage, and
because of her fever she's a little less than coherent.

>   JOYCE
>   Buffy? Hi, sweetheart.
>
>   XANDER
>   Hey, Buffy. We're all here.
>
>   BUFFY
>   (slurring her words)
>   Heyyy... here were are. It's all of
>   we! Are we taking me home?

Buffy tries to sit up.

>   DR. WILKINSON
>   Buffy, you need to lie down.
>
>   BUFFY
>   (protesting weakly)
>   Yes, lie at home. My bed is better
>   than any bed that's not my bed.
>
>   DR. WILKINSON
>   (to the others)
>   She's still a little out of it.

CONTINUED

4 CONTINUED: 4

                    BUFFY
          Shhh! Hospital zone. No singing.

     Dr. Wilkinson gently pushes Buffy back down.

                    DR. WILKINSON
          She'll feel better after she's been
          here a while.

     Buffy, suddenly sober, begins struggling with the covers.

                    BUFFY
          No. Let me go.

                    WILLOW
          Buffy, what's wrong?

                    BUFFY
              (fighting more)
          Let me go!

                    CORDELIA
          I think she wants to go.

                    DR. WILKINSON
              (calling out)
          I need some assistance!

     A FEW NURSES rush over and help subdue Buffy, who is in major
     freak mode.

                    BUFFY
          Giles, tell them. The vampires.
          I've got to kill the vampires!

                    JOYCE
          Vampires?

     Dr. Wilkinson prepares a syringe.

                    DR. WILKINSON
          She's been like this since she came
          in.

                    XANDER
              (covering)
          Probably the fever?

                    WILLOW
          Yeah. It's made her delusional.

                                                              CONTINUED

4 CONTINUED: (2) 4

> BUFFY
> (frantic)
> They're out there!

Giles laughs nervously.

> GILES
> It's okay, Buffy. We'll get those vampires some other time!
> (off Joyce's look)
> I hear it's best to just go along.

> DR. WILKINSON
> This will help her relax.

The nurses hold Buffy down as Dr. Wilkinson gives her a shot. Joyce leans down to her daughter.

> JOYCE
> Honey...?

> BUFFY
> (frail)
> I want to go home.

> JOYCE
> (taking her hand)
> Everything's going to be okay. I promise.

Buffy STARES up from the gurney as her eyes get heavy from the sedative.

> BUFFY
> (fights to stay awake)
> Please don't make me stay. Not here.

Buffy is wheeled into a room as the gang waits in the hall. They watch Buffy through the window.

> XANDER
> That was a new experience. I'm not used to seeing Buffy scared like that.

> JOYCE
> She just hates hospitals. Since she was a little girl.

> WILLOW
> What happened?

CONTINUED

4   CONTINUED: (3)   4

>   JOYCE
>   (tentatively)
>   When Buffy was eight... her cousin,
>   Celia, died in a hospital.
>   (a beat)
>   Buffy was alone with her when it
>   happened.
>
>   CORDELIA
>   (sadly)
>   Yuck.
>
>   JOYCE
>   They were very close.
>
>   WILLOW
>   And she was eight?
>
>   JOYCE
>   She doesn't talk about it, but... she
>   just doesn't like hospitals.
>
>   XANDER
>   Can't say as I blame.

She stares in at Buffy.

>   JOYCE
>   Looks like she's asleep. I should go
>   call her father.
>
>   GILES
>   I think there's a phone...

Joyce goes off with Giles.

>   JOYCE
>   Thank you for coming. I really
>   appreciate the way you look out for
>   her. All of you.
>
>   GILES
>   We're very fond of her.
>
>   JOYCE
>   (pauses, gathering)
>   I hope I'm not out of line, but I
>   just wanted to say how sorry I am
>   about that teacher, Ms. Calendar.
>   Buffy said you were close.

                                                          CONTINUED

4 CONTINUED: (4)   4

>   GILES
>   Thank you.
>
>   JOYCE
>   Buffy's been so down since it
>   happened. She _never_ gets sick.
>
>   GILES
>   I'm sure she'll be fine.
>
>   JOYCE
>   I'm sorry, I babble when I'm nervous.
>   I just wanted to -- well, if you need
>   anything.

ANGLE: THE OTHERS

Looking into Buffy's room.

>   XANDER
>   You think she'll be okay in here?
>
>   CORDELIA
>   I don't know... Lysette got her nose
>   done here, you know; she asked for
>   the Gwyneth Paltrow but it looked
>   more like the Mr. Potato Head --
>
>   XANDER
>   Cordy.
>
>   WILLOW
>   Buffy's not here for cosmetic surgery.
>
>   CORDELIA
>   No, but while she's here she could
>   get that thing taken care of. That
>   thing on her face -- you know, that
>   _thing_.
>
>   WILLOW
>   Do you think Angel would attack her
>   in here?
>
>   XANDER
>   He can come in. It's a public
>   building.
>
>   WILLOW
>   That's true...

*

                                                              CONTINUED

BUFFY THE VAMPIRE SLAYER "Killed By Death" (WHITE) 2/2/98   14.

4   CONTINUED: (5)   4

   They start off.

                       CORDELIA
             Am I the only one who's noticed that
             thing?

   CAMERA MOVES IN ON BUFFY and we:

                                              MATCH DISSOLVE TO:

5   INT. BUFFY'S HOSPITAL ROOM - LATER THAT NIGHT   5

   An IV DRIP courses through a tube connected to Buffy's arm.
   She TOSSES and TURNS, sleeping fitfully. She MOANS
   occasionally, drifting in and out of consciousness.

   She OPENS HER EYES with a start and sees a little boy
   standing in the doorway, staring at her. His name is RYAN.
   He's still, expressionless, Stepfordian. Think Christopher
   Walken at age ten.

   He walks away.

   Suddenly, a MYSTERIOUS FIGURE passes by the door, following
   the boy. The figure is tall, not quite human, dressed in
   dark clothes -- like an eighteenth-century undertaker.

   In the dark, Buffy barely registers the figure's GHASTLY
   WHITE FACE, BEAK-LIKE NOSE, HAIRLESS HEAD, and UGLY RED-
   RIMMED EYES.

   And just as quickly as the figure appeared, it's GONE. Buffy
   gets out of bed, UNHOOKS the IV, and heads out the door.

                                                     FLASH TO:

6   INT. DIFFERENT HOSPITAL - NINE YEARS AGO (NIGHT)   6

   HAZY DREAM-CAM:

   An EIGHT-YEAR-OLD GIRL (who looks as much like an eight-year-
   old Sarah as Marcia can find) comes out of a room. This is
   LITTLE BUFFY. She slowly and tentatively walks down the
   middle of a HARSHLY LIT hospital corridor. MOANS ECHO
   throughout the hall as Little Buffy looks around.

   FROM HER POV, everything seems heightened and menacing --
   shapes are distorted, voices are muffled, etc.

                                                     CONTINUED

BUFFY THE VAMPIRE SLAYER "Killed By Death" (WHITE) 2/2/98   15.

6   CONTINUED: 6

    Little Buffy passes by various things in the hallway: an
    EMPTY WHEELCHAIR... a cart on which sits a TRAY of SURGICAL
    INSTRUMENTS... a defibrillator 'CRASH CART'....

    She PEERS INTO A ROOM and sees a CURTAIN pulled around a bed.
    Little Buffy cautiously heads into the room...

7   INT. DIFFERENT HOSP. ROOM - CONT.(NINE YEARS AGO; NIGHT)   7

    ...and walks toward the curtain. She nervously REACHES to
    pull it away. When she TOUCHES it--

    A FLASH fills the screen and we are back in:

8   INT. BUFFY'S HOSPITAL ROOM - NIGHT (PRESENT DAY)   8

    BUFFY WAKES UP in her hospital bed. The room is dark. She
    looks around, disoriented, getting her bearings. The clock
    next to her bed reads 2:27 AM.

    She SITS UP and feels something tug at her arm.

                        BUFFY
                Ow...

    She looks to see that the IV is still connected.

    The FAINT SOUND of CHILDREN CRYING can be heard from down the
    hall. The sound only adds to Buffy's visible despair.

    She unhooks the IV from her arm, throws her covers off, and
    gets out of bed. She STEADIES herself on the bed rail, takes
    a breath, and heads into the hallway.

9   INT. SUNNYDALE HOSPITAL CORRIDOR - CONTINUOUS (NIGHT)   9

    The hospital is eerily deserted.

    Buffy makes her way down the hall. She looks into rooms and
    sees PATIENTS lying in beds, hooked up to monitors,
    ventilators at work, etc.

    A SECURITY GUARD (DON: more on him later) skulks around,
    watching her. Buffy turns down another hallway, following
    the sounds of the crying.

BUFFY THE VAMPIRE SLAYER "Killed By Death" (WHITE) 2/2/98   16.

10 INT. SUNNYDALE HOSPITAL - ANOTHER CORRIDOR - CONT.(NIGHT)   10

As Buffy rounds a corner, she sees a couple of ORDERLIES wheeling a gurney into the hallway. On the gurney is a SMALL, SHEET-COVERED BODY.

She goes to a door and looks inside.

11 INT. SUNNYDALE HOSPITAL KIDS' WARD - CONT. (NIGHT)   11

This is the kids' ward -- a half dozen or so beds and a dreary collection of medical equipment. Second-hand stuffed animals and faded posters of clowns are supposed to add life to the depressing room.

A few of the CHILDREN sleep restlessly as machines monitor their conditions.

Dr. Wilkinson is arguing with another doctor (DR. STANLEY BACKER), an elderly man with disheveled hair and a manner that's just a bit off-kilter.

>			DR. WILKINSON
> I'm just saying step back the dosage until we can analyze the results.
>
>			DR. BACKER
> There isn't time. I would think that would be clear by now.
>
>			DR. WILKINSON
> The normal course of treatment --
>
>			DR. BACKER
> They aren't responding to the normal course of treatment. They're getting worse.

As they talk, he takes a hypo of fluid, injects it into a child's IV.

>			DR. WILKINSON
> Raising their temperatures is potentially --
>
>			DR. BACKER
> Dr. Wilkinson, I have the parents' consent.
>
>			DR. WILKINSON
> They're desperate. They don't understand what you're doing.

CONTINUED

BUFFY THE VAMPIRE SLAYER "Killed By Death" (WHITE) 2/2/98   17.

11   CONTINUED: 11

                    DR. BACKER
          If you have a problem with my
          methods, bring it up with the board.

                    DR. WILKINSON
          I have.

Buffy backs away and BUMPS into someone.

Ryan, the Christopher Walken boy, stands there, holding the
hand of a LITTLE GIRL.

                    RYAN
          He comes at night. The grown-ups
          don't see him.

Buffy looks at Ryan, confused.

                    RYAN (cont'd)
          He was with Tina. He'll come back
          for us.

                    BUFFY
          Who?

                    RYAN
          Death.

                                                        BLACK OUT.

               END OF ACT ONE

ACT TWO

12 INT. SUNNYDALE HOSPITAL ENTRANCE AREA - NIGHT   12

The middle of the night. Not too many people. A NURSE or
two. Maybe a JANITOR. A couple of COPS talk to an apparent
ASSAULT VICTIM who holds an ice pack to his head.

ANGLE: A BOUQUET OF FLOWERS

as someone enters from the outside carrying them.

It's Angel. He saunters past the reception desk -- only to
have Xander step in his path.

                    XANDER
          Visiting hours are over.

                    ANGEL
          Well, I'm pretty much family.

                    XANDER
          Why don't you come back during the
          day... Or, gee, no. I guess you
          can't.

                    ANGEL
          If I decide to walk into Buffy's room
          do you think for one microsecond that
          you could stop me?

                    XANDER
          Maybe not. Maybe that security guard
          couldn't either -- or those cops. Or
          all the orderlies... I'm kind of
          curious to find out. You game?

                    ANGEL
          Buffy's white knight. You still love
          her. It must just eat you up that I
          got there first.   *

Xander clenches his jaw against the truth of it.

                    XANDER
          You're gonna die. I'm gonna be there.

Angel smiles, hands Xander the flowers.

                    ANGEL
          Tell her I stopped by.

                                                    CONTINUED

BUFFY THE VAMPIRE SLAYER "Killed By Death" (WHITE) 2/2/98   19.

12 CONTINUED: 12

He exits, Xander suddenly shaky with released fear and tension.

                                        DISSOLVE TO:

13 INT. BEDROOM - NINE YEARS AGO (NIGHT)   13

CLOSE-ON:

The face of an eight-year-old girl (CELIA), who WHIMPERS and CRIES OUT in distress.

                    CELIA
            Help me... Help!

PULL BACK to see that the girl is underneath a pile of PILLOWS and we are in a little girl's bedroom. The girl is play-acting.

                    CELIA (cont'd)
            Avalanche! Help! Help! I'm trapped!

Little Buffy appears in the doorway, hands on her hips. A bedspread serves as a makeshift cape.

                    LITTLE BUFFY
            Power Girl to the rescue!

Little Buffy runs over and, with 'superhuman strength,' lifts the huge 'boulders' off of Celia.

                    CELIA
            You saved me! Thank you, Power Girl!

                    LITTLE BUFFY
            You're safe now.

A FLASH fills the screen and we are in:

14 INT. DIFFERENT HOSPITAL ROOM - NINE YEARS AGO (NIGHT)   14

HAZY DREAM-CAM:

As before -- Little Buffy PULLS the curtain aside, glimpsing the small FEET, then LEGS and BODY of a child lying in bed.

Another FLASH and we:

                                        CUT TO:

15 INT. BUFFY'S HOSPITAL ROOM - DAY (PRESENT DAY)   15

Buffy WAKES with a start. Dr. Wilkinson stares down at her.

          DR. WILKINSON
Good morning.

          BUFFY
Coulda fooled me...

          DR. WILKINSON
How are you feeling?
     (off chart)
Looks like your fever is down.

          BUFFY
     (rising)
Well, good. Thanks for having me and let's try to keep in touch.

          DR. WILKINSON
Not so fast.

She pushes Buffy gently back down, checking her arm.

          DR. WILKINSON (cont'd)
Hmmm.

          BUFFY
Good Hmmm or bad Hmmm?

          DR. WILKINSON
Swelling is down... Swelling is gone. Does that hurt?

          BUFFY
Nope.

          DR. WILKINSON
Amazing...

          BUFFY
So I should go.

          DR. WILKINSON
Soon. We want to make sure that fever's gone. It's a strong virus. Not as strong as *you*, maybe...

          BUFFY
Is that what Tina had?

                        CONTINUED

15 CONTINUED: 15

Dr. Wilkinson looks down. Before she can answer, Giles, Willow, Xander and Cordelia enter.

> GILES
> May we come in?

> DR. WILKINSON
> Please. See if you can keep our patient from bolting.
>   (to Buffy)
> Rest.

Dr. Wilkinson heads out as Giles, Xander, Willow, and Cordelia come in. Xander presents a balloon bouquet to Buffy.

> XANDER
> Flowers for m'lady?

> BUFFY
> These are balloons.

> XANDER
> Stick 'em in water, maybe they'll grow.

> WILLOW
> And, not to be outdone--

She grandly presents Buffy with a pile of:

> BUFFY
> Homework.

> WILLOW
> Just my way of saying 'Get Well Soon.'

> BUFFY
> You know, chocolate says that even better.

> WILLOW
> I did all of your assignments. All you have to do is sign your name.

> BUFFY
>   (awestruck)
> Chocolate means nothing to me.

Cordelia fidgets.

CONTINUED

15 CONTINUED: (2)   15

                    CORDELIA
          Nobody told me we were supposed to
          bring gifts. I was out of the loop
          on gifts.

                    GILES
          Well, it's traditional among...
          people.
                    (to Buffy)
          Did you pass the night well enough?

                    BUFFY
          Well, not really. Some stuff
          happened, I'm wondering...

She looks into the crowded hall.

                    BUFFY (cont'd)
          Let's take a walk.

                                                          CUT TO:

16 EXT. SUNNYDALE HOSPITAL COURTYARD - DAY   16

Willow pushes Buffy in a wheelchair as the gang walks along.

                    BUFFY
          Now this part I could get used to.

                    WILLOW
          You want me to go real fast?
                    (off Giles' look)
          Not that I would...

                    GILES
                    (to Buffy)
          You were discussing 'stuff'?

                    BUFFY
          Stuff, yeah. You know a girl died
          here last night.

                    WILLOW
          How?

                    BUFFY
          Well, that flu.

                                                          CONTINUED

16 CONTINUED: 16

                    XANDER
          Flu? Doesn't exactly sound
          monsterrific.

                    BUFFY
          Well, there's this Dr. Backer, he's
          been giving them experimental
          treatments -- he's kinda creepy --
          I'm not sure what he's up to. And
          then I met this kid, Ryan. He said
          he saw something.

                    GILES
          Saw what?

                    BUFFY
          Death.

                    CORDELIA
          Death?

                    WILLOW
          The Death? As in, 'it is your time?'

                    GILES
          Buffy, a frightened child --

                    BUFFY
          But I thought I saw something -- I
          was out of it, I'm not sure, but.

                    CORDELIA
          But you do know it was death?

                    WILLOW
          Did he have an hourglass?

                    XANDER
          If he asks you to play chess, don't
          even do it. Guy's like a whiz.

                    BUFFY
          Look, maybe it wasn't death.
               (pointedly)
          Maybe it was something else.

                                                              CONTINUED

16 CONTINUED: (2)   16

                    CORDELIA
          Okay, so this isn't about that you're
          afraid of hospitals cause your little
          friend died and you wanna conjure up
          a monster that you can fight and save
          everybody and not feel helpless?

                    GILES
          Cordelia, have you ever actually
          <u>heard</u> of tact?

                    CORDELIA
          Tact is just not saying true stuff.
          I'll pass.

                    WILLOW
               (to Buffy)
          Your mom did tell us about your
          cousin...

                    BUFFY
          This has nothing to do with that.   *
          This kid Ryan was afraid of   *
          something. Something real. As long   *
          as I'm forced to stay here, I wanna
          find out what.

                    XANDER
          Is this the place where we say, 'What
          can we do to help?'

17 INT. SUNNYDALE HOSP. RECORDS ROOM - A WHILE LATER (DAY)   17

                    CORDELIA
          You had to ask that, didn't you?

Cordelia and Xander have opened the door to a medium-sized
room. File cabinets line every wall. On the front of the
door: 'MEDICAL RECORDS ROOM - AUTHORIZED PERSONNEL ONLY.'

                    XANDER
          It'll be cake. We find out exactly
          how this little girl Tina died, we
          get out. Five minutes, tops.

                    CORDELIA
          This is what happens when you try to
          be compassionate toward sick people.
          They take advantage of you.

                                                    CONTINUED

17 CONTINUED: 17

> XANDER
> Mm-hmm. Buffy almost died just so she could put you out.
>
> CORDELIA
> I didn't want to be the first one to say it.
>
> XANDER
> (pointing)
> Me here, you there.
>
> CORDELIA
> Right.

Xander checks one side of the room as Cordelia goes to a row of file cabinets. She scans the cabinets, then reaches for a drawer. A HAND GRABS hers. She screams. A goofy, yet menacing-looking security guard (Don, the guard Buffy saw in the hallway) stands there.

> DON
> What are you doing here?

CUT TO:

18 INT. LIBRARY - DAY   18

Giles and Willow come through the doors.

> WILLOW
> Okay, where do we start?
>
> GILES
> Hmm? Oh, I don't know. Maybe look into the history of the hospital, bizarre incidents, that sort of thing.
>
> WILLOW
> I'm sensing less than full committal here.
>
> GILES
> Well, I suppose... Cordelia may be Homerically Insensitive, but she may also be right. Disease and death are things -- possibly the only things-- that Buffy cannot fight.
> (more)

CONTINUED

18 CONTINUED: 18

                    GILES (cont'd)
          It would be natural for her to try to
          create a defeatable opponent.
          Especially now, after... after Jenny.

                    WILLOW
          That's true. But, on the we-live-on-
          the-Hellmouth side, these kids might
          have seen a monster.

                    GILES
          That no grown-up can see. Doesn't
          ring a bell. Unless...

                    WILLOW
          Unless?

                    GILES
          Sometimes small children do see
          something we adults don't. Us. Our
          true selves. Our hidden faces.

                    WILLOW
          So the kids might be afraid of a
          regular person. Like the weird
          doctor.

                    GILES
          Stanley Backer was the name, no?   *

                    WILLOW
                (turns to the
                  computer)
          Let's look him up.

19 INT. SUNNYDALE HOSPITAL RECORDS ROOM - SAME TIME (DAY)   19

     Cordelia stares 'admiringly' at Don as he brags to her.

                    DON
          You know, people always think
          security guards are just guys that
          failed the police exam. That's not
          me -- this is my career.

                    CORDELIA
          Stereotypes are so unfair.

                                                           CONTINUED

19 CONTINUED: 19

                    DON
          I did take the fireman exam, though.
          I didn't do so good.

                    CORDELIA
          I think security guards are way
          sexier than firemen. They're all so
          sooty.

                    DON
          This is where the action is, anyhow.
          I'm all the time restraining people.

                    CORDELIA
          Ooh, how thrilling. Do you get
          scared?

                    DON
          'Fear is for the weak.' That's my
          motto. Well, either that or 'Live in
          the now.' I haven't decided yet.

                    CORDELIA
          I bet you see a lot of tragedy, too.
          Like that little girl...

                    DON
          One of Dr. Backer's patients. Dr.
          Backer's a great man. He understands
          the real truth about children.

                    CORDELIA
          What's that?

                    DON
          Sometimes they die.

Cordy tries to hide her expression. Don's haughty schoolboy bravado is suddenly laced with creepy.

Xander moves away from the cabinet and accidentally KICKS a drawer. Don looks up and whips out his BILLY CLUB.

                    DON (cont'd)
          What was that?

                    CORDELIA
          I didn't hear anything.

Don holds his hand out to quiet her. Cordelia TENSES. Xander is about to be busted, when Cordelia blurts out:

                                                    CONTINUED

19 CONTINUED: (2)   19

                    CORDELIA (cont'd)
               You have got the most perfect nose I
               have ever seen.

Don turns back.

                    CORDELIA (cont'd)
               You must work out.

Behind Don, Xander WAVES a file at Cordelia, and escapes out
the open door.

20 INT. SUNNYDALE HOSPITAL CORRIDOR - CONTINUOUS (DAY)   20

Xander comes out of the records room and stands in the
hallway, flipping through the file. After a few seconds,
Cordelia comes out.

                    XANDER
               Could you make just a little more
               with the touchy-gropey?

                    CORDELIA
               Jealous?

                    XANDER
               Of Rogain boy? I don't think so.
                    (hands her the file)
               Take this to Giles, okay?

                    CORDELIA
               What about you?

                    XANDER
               I'm staying here.

                    CORDELIA
               Oh, right, your obsession with
               protecting Buffy. Have I ever told
               you how attractive that's not?

                    XANDER
               Cordelia, someone's gotta watch her
               back.

                    CORDELIA
               Yeah, I've seen you watch her 'back.'

                    XANDER
               What's that supposed to mean?

                                                      CONTINUED

20 CONTINUED: 20

                    CORDELIA
                (calmly explains)
            I was using the phrase 'watch her
            back' as a euphemism for looking at
            her butt. Sort of a pun.

                    XANDER
            Oh. Right. Hey!

                    CORDELIA
                (angry again)
            Well, you do!

                    XANDER
            Jealous?

                    CORDELIA
            Fine. Watch my back.

As she turns it on him and storms out. He watches her go,
irked -- his eyes drift down for a moment, appreciative --
then back up, irked.

21 INT. LIBRARY - LATER THAT NIGHT   21

Willow and Giles are looking at the computer.

                    GILES
            The good Doctor Backer has something
            of a rap sheet.

                    WILLOW
                (off computer)
            Reprimands for controversial
            experiments, risky procedures -- a
            malpractice suit... looks like it was
            dropped suddenly.

                    GILES
            Factor in Buffy's observation that
            he, uh, gives her the wiggins...

                    WILLOW
            This could be our death guy?

                    GILES
            I just wish I knew what he was doing
            to these children.

                                                    DISSOLVE TO:

22 INT. DR. BACKER'S OFFICE - LATER (NIGHT)   22

A dark office with degrees on the wall, shelves of medical books, a small refrigerator, etc.

Dr. Backer pores over a number of reports. He OPENS the refrigerator and pulls out a couple of VIALS marked with different colored labels. He SCRIBBLES something on one of the vials, then rifles through a stack of files. He opens one and double checks his facts. He smiles.

                    DR. BACKER
          Yes...

He excitedly WRITES some notes in the file.

                                               DISSOLVE TO:

23 INT. SUNNYDALE HOSPITAL ENTRANCE AREA - NIGHT   23

Xander is on watch again. He slumps in a chair, bored and tired.

A BAG OF DONUTS falls into frame on the table before him.

Cordelia places two coffees on the table as she sits by Xander. He looks at her briefly, then goes for a coffee, sips it as Cordy opens a Cosmo, quietly reads.

24 INT. SUNNYDALE HOSPITAL KIDS' WARD - NIGHT   24

Most of the kids are in their beds reading, playing with toys, etc. Buffy comes in, looks around, and sees Ryan at a small table, coloring on a pad. She goes over to him.

                    BUFFY
          Hi. Remember me?

                    RYAN
          You're not supposed to be here.

                    BUFFY
          Why not?

                    RYAN
          Contagious.

                    BUFFY
          Oh, I already got what you got.

He shakes his head.

                                                    CONTINUED

BUFFY THE VAMPIRE SLAYER "Killed By Death" (WHITE) 2/2/98   31.

24 CONTINUED: 24

                    BUFFY (cont'd)
            What, 'cause I'm a grown-up? Believe
            me, I'm not that grown-up --

    She stops, looking at his picture.

    CLOSE-UP of the crayon drawing. Buffy has seen this thing
    before.

                                        FLASH TO:

25 INT. BUFFY'S HOSPITAL ROOM - THE NIGHT BEFORE   25

    A REPLAY from last night. Ryan stands in the doorway. The
    pale-visaged fiend passes behind, this time in SLOW MOTION.

                                        FLASH TO:

26 INT. SUNNYDALE HOSP. KIDS' WARD - BACK TO PRESENT (NIGHT)   26

    Buffy stares at the drawing. It's almost a perfect likeness
    of the creepy creature.

                    RYAN
            He'll come again tonight.

                    BUFFY
            Ryan, listen to me. I'm not gonna
            let this thing hurt you. Any of you.

    He is silent.

                    BUFFY (cont'd)
            Grown-ups don't believe you, right?
            I do. There are real monsters, we
            both know that. But there're real
            heroes, too, that fight monsters.
            That's me.

                    RYAN
            Can't fight death.

                                        DISSOLVE TO:

27 INT. SUNNYDALE HOSPITAL CORRIDOR - NIGHT   27

    The hallways are eerily DESERTED.

                                                     CONTINUED

BUFFY THE VAMPIRE SLAYER "Killed By Death" (WHITE) 2/2/98   32.

27 CONTINUED: 27

Dr. Backer comes out of his office and walks down the hall.
Buffy STEPS OUT of the shadows, where she has been waiting
and watching.

28 INT. SUNNYDALE HOSP. KIDS' WARD - A MOMENT LATER (NIGHT)   28

The room is dark. The kids are asleep. Dr. Backer quietly
comes into the room. He goes over to one of the kids.

CLOSE ON: THE CHILD, sleeping peacefully.

Dr. Backer holds a syringe up to the light and pushes some of
the serum out the top. He disconnects the kid's IV, INJECTS
the tube with serum, then re-connects the IV.

Buffy appears in the doorway as Dr. Backer finishes his job.
As he turns to move to the next bed, Buffy MOVES out of his
sight-line, hiding in the hallway.

Dr. Backer leans towards another SLEEPING CHILD, when:

He hears a NOISE. He looks around, sees nothing, then goes
back to his work.

Suddenly, Dr. Backer is SLASHED across the arm by an
invisible CLAW. He starts to CRY OUT, but an unseen hand
CLAMPS over his throat, muffling his voice.   *

We HEAR another SLICE (his stomach, which is below camera
view) and his face contorts in pain. The unseen force then
THROWS him towards the door --

29 INT. SUNNYDALE HOSPITAL CORRIDOR - CONTINUOUS (NIGHT)   29

--and Dr. Backer's body comes TUMBLING out, right past Buffy.

Dr. Backer lies on the ground, unmoving. Dead. Buffy goes
to him and starts to kneel down when:

She is THROWN ASIDE by the invisible force. She SLAMS
against a wall and FALLS to the ground, dazed.

Dr. Backer's arms are LIFTED UP, and his body begins to move
as the unseen thing DRAGS him past Buffy and AROUND A CORNER.

                          BLACK OUT.

                        END OF ACT TWO

BUFFY THE VAMPIRE SLAYER "Killed By Death" (WHITE) 2/2/98

ACT THREE

30 EXT. SUNNYDALE HOSPITAL - THE NEXT DAY

To establish the morning.

31 INT. BUFFY'S HOSPITAL ROOM - CONTINUOUS (DAY)

Giles, Xander, Willow, and Cordelia come in to find Buffy sitting on the bed.

> GILES
> Well. It looks like you were on to something after all.

> BUFFY
> I know.

> GILES
> The girl Tina -- it looks as though she died from the fever, simple enough. But her records show her improving and then suddenly worsening without apparent cause.

> WILLOW
> So we checked out Dr. Backer and this guy is not the solid citizen --

> BUFFY
> It's not him. Backer was clean.

> CORDELIA
> What do you mean, clean?

> XANDER
> What do you mean, was?

> BUFFY
> (shows Ryan's picture)
> He's dead. This thing killed him. And not with kindness.

> WILLOW
> You saw it.

CONTINUED

31 CONTINUED: 31

                    BUFFY
          No, it was invisible. I saw Backer
          nearly shredded and the thing knocked
          me down. It's real. Which means I
          get to fight it.

                    GILES
          It would help if you knew what it
          was. It's invisible to you but the
          children can see it.

                    CORDELIA
          But you said you did see something
          the other night.

                    BUFFY
          Yeah, but I was pretty delirious...
          I mean, why would I see it then and
          not last night?

Joyce enters, smiling.

                    JOYCE
          Good morning. Ooh, it looks like I
          interrupted a secret meeting.

Giles emits a fake laugh.

                    CORDELIA
          You sure didn't, though.

                    JOYCE
               (to Buffy)
          Honey, I just talked to the doctor.
          She says I can take you home.

For a beat, nobody speaks.

                    BUFFY
          I have to stay here.

                    JOYCE
          Stay? But honey, I thought --

                    BUFFY
          I think my symptoms are flaring up
          again.

                    WILLOW
          She doesn't look well.

                                              CONTINUED

31 CONTINUED: (2) 31

> BUFFY
> 'Cause I'm not well. I feel oogy.

> XANDER
> Increased oogy-ness... That's a danger signal.

> JOYCE
> Are you sure?

> BUFFY
> Yeah. Just for another day...

> JOYCE
> Well, I'll talk to the doctor.

She leaves, a tad bemused.

> XANDER
> What's the drill?

> BUFFY
> (hands Giles the picture)
> Giles, let's get a mug shot on this guy. I kneed to know who I'm fighting.

> GILES
> Right.

> BUFFY
> I'll check Backer's office. See if there are any post-its marked 'Why a monster might want me dead.'

> XANDER
> SoundS like a plan.

> BUFFY
> If I do find something, I probably won't have the slightest idea what it means, so, Willow...

> WILLOW
> Oh, I'm good with medical stuff. Xander and I used to play doctor all the time.

CONTINUED

31 CONTINUED: (3)   31

                    XANDER
               (off their looks)
          No, she's being literal. She had all
          these medical volumes, used to
          diagnose me with stuff. I didn't
          have the heart to tell her she was
          playing it wrong.

                    WILLOW
          Wrong? Why?
               (to Buffy)
          How did you play doctor?

                    BUFFY
               (lying, embarrassed)
          I never have.

                    GILES
          Fascinating though this is...

                    BUFFY
          Yeah. Right. Go.

                    GILES
          We'll call when we know something.

                    BUFFY
          Know something soon.

32 INT. SUNNYDALE HOSPITAL CORRIDOR - CONTINUOUS (DAY)   32

     Giles, Xander and Cordelia come out of Buffy's room.

                    GILES
          I'd best head for the library.
          Research beckons.

                    XANDER
          I'm on sentry duty. Angel won't show
          'til sundown if at all, but maybe
          I'll get lucky with this death guy.

                    CORDELIA
          He's invisible.

                    XANDER
          Yeah, but if I see a floating pipe
          and smoking jacket, he's dropped.

                                                        CONTINUED

32 CONTINUED: 32

      GILES
  Well, keep alert, you two.

      XANDER
  Finding out who this thing is is the
  priority. Cordy, you should go with
  Giles.

      GILES
    (petulant)
  But why do I have to have --
    (stops himself)
  Good thinking. I could use a
  research assistant.

      CORDELIA
    (dead pan look)
  Let's go, tact-guy.
    (to Xander)
  Be careful.

Cordelia and Giles walk off. Xander heads in the other direction.

           DISSOLVE TO:

A33 INT. SUNNYDALE HOSPITAL KIDS' WARD - NIGHT A33

The door opens and Ryan looks out into the hall, silent and conspiratorial. He sees Don standing, idle, nearby. He lets the door shut again, slowly.

33 INT. DR. BACKER'S OFFICE - A LITTLE LATER (DAY) 33

The office is empty. Dark. Eerie. Just as Dr. Backer left it the night before. The DOOR opens; Buffy and Willow come inside.

They move inside and shut the door. Buffy TURNS ON THE LIGHTS; they look around.

      WILLOW
  It's weird going through his stuff.
  He didn't finish his coffee. Guess
  he won't.

She sees a folder, starts leafing through it.

           CONTINUED

33 CONTINUED: 33

                        BUFFY
            Yet another person I wasn't in time
            to save. I wish Angel had put me in
            the hospital sooner.
                (pauses)
            There's a sentence I never expected
            to say.

                        WILLOW
            I think I got something here.

                        BUFFY
            Yeah?

She opens the folder and starts leafing through the contents
as Buffy searches around the room.

                        WILLOW
            Okay, this makes sense... Dr. Backer
            was trying to inoculate kids with
            a controlled dosage of the same virus
            they already had. Raising their
            temperatures to burn the fever out of
            them.

Buffy opens the refrigerator; pulls out a couple of VIALS
marked with different colored labels.

                        BUFFY
            Would that work?

                        WILLOW
                (looking at charts)
            According to this, it was starting
            to. So he really was helping the
            kids.

CLOSE-ON: Ryan's drawing.

                        BUFFY (V.O.)
            Until that thing stopped him.

34 OMITTED   34

35 INT. LIBRARY - NIGHT   35

PULL BACK from the drawing to see Giles is comparing it to
illustrations in a book (sort of a mug book for phantoms and
demons) looking for a match. Cordelia peruses another book.

                                                              CONTINUED

35 CONTINUED: 35

   Giles turns page after page; Cordelia lingers on each one.
   (His stack of books dwarfs hers.)

                        CORDELIA
              Ew. What's this one do?

                        GILES
              What?
                   (looks over, annoyed)
              Oh. It, um, extracts vital internal
              organs so that it can regenerate its
              own mutating cells.

                        CORDELIA
              Wow.
                   (turns a page)
              What's this one do?

                        GILES
                   (lets out a breath)
              It elongates its mouth to engulf the
              head of its casualty between its
              teeth.

                        CORDELIA
              Ouch.
                   (turns a page)
              What's this one do?

                        GILES
                   (fed up)
              It asks endless questions of those
              with whom it's supposed to be working
              but they're not getting anything done!

                        CORDELIA
              Boy, there's a demon for everything.

   Giles pushes his book aside; frustrated.

                        GILES
              I'm not even sure we're going down
              the right track. Since this
              miscreant is only seen by select
              individuals, there's a chance we
              won't ever find a picture of it.

   Cordelia finishes paging through a book.

                        CORDELIA
              Well, it's not in here.

                                                        CONTINUED

35 CONTINUED: (2)   35

She closes the book. There, ON THE COVER, is the MONSTER.

                                        CUT TO:

36 INT. LIBRARY - A MOMENT LATER (NIGHT)   36

Cordelia holds the book as she speaks into the phone.

     CORDELIA
  It's called 'Der Kindestod.'

37 INT. BUFFY'S HOSPITAL ROOM - SAME TIME (NIGHT)   37

Willow stands next to Buffy, who speaks into the phone.

     BUFFY
  Who is this?

38 INT. BUFFY'S HOSPITAL ROOM/INT. LIBRARY - CONTINUOUS   38

WE INTERCUT BETWEEN THE TWO THROUGHOUT THE CONVERSATION.

     CORDELIA
  It's me. I got your monster.

Buffy gives Willow a strange look.

     BUFFY
     (confused)
  Where's Giles?

     CORDELIA
  Looking up stuff.

     BUFFY
  Well, can you put him on?

     CORDELIA
  Hey, I found this Kindestod guy.
  Just listen.

     BUFFY
  Right.

                                        CONTINUED

38 CONTINUED: 38

>   CORDELIA
>   The name means 'Child Death.' This
>   book says he feeds off of children by
>   sucking the life out of them. Blech.
>   But afterwards, it just looks like
>   they died because they were sick.
>
>   BUFFY
>   So it <u>did</u> kill Tina?
>
>   CORDELIA
>   That's my take. 'Cause it would be
>   looking at that children's ward as
>   basically an all-you-can-eat kind of
>   thing.
>
>   BUFFY
>   Backer was curing the kids -- and
>   taking away the Kindestod's food.
>
>   CORDELIA
>   Hence the slice-age.

Giles comes over to Cordelia holding another book.

>   GILES
>   I found a picture of how it kills.
>   Let me talk to--

Cordelia snatches the book out of his hand and looks at the picture (which we cannot see). She reacts disgusted into the phone.

>   CORDELIA
>   EWW!
>
>   BUFFY
>   What?
>
>   CORDELIA
>   You should see how this thing does
>   its things! I mean... ewww!

She doesn't want a part of this. She hands the book and the phone to Giles.

>   CORDELIA (cont'd)
>   I don't know why you dragged me here.

Giles takes the phone.

                                                          CONTINUED

38 CONTINUED: (2)   38

                    GILES
          Buffy, you still there?

                    BUFFY
          Hanging on every 'ew.'

                    GILES
                (off picture)
          The Kindestod gorges by sitting atop
          his prey, pinning it down helplessly.
          Then he slowly draws out the life.
          It must be horrifying for the victim.
                (a beat)
          Buffy?

39 INT. BUFFY'S HOSPITAL ROOM - SAME TIME (NIGHT)   39

    Buffy is silent, staring off into space.

                    GILES (O.C.)
          Hello?

    A FLASH fills the screen and we are:

40 INT. DIFFERENT HOSPITAL ROOM - NINE YEARS AGO (NIGHT)   40

    HAZY DREAM-CAM:

    Little Buffy finishes pulling the curtain all the way back.
    She sees her cousin Celia lying in bed, GASPING and PANTING
    as she is PINNED DOWN by an invisible force.

                    LITTLE BUFFY
          Celia?

    Little Buffy approaches closer. Suddenly, Celia shoots out
    her hand and GRABS Little Buffy's wrist tightly. Terror
    covers Celia's face as she struggles for breath.

                    LITTLE BUFFY (cont'd)
          What's wrong?

                    CELIA
          Get it off me! Get it off me!

    Little Buffy looks on, horrified.

                    LITTLE BUFFY
          I don't know what to do! Celia!

                                                              CONTINUED

40 CONTINUED: 40

The screen FADES TO WHITE and then to:

41 INT. BUFFY'S HOSPITAL ROOM - PRESENT DAY (NIGHT)   41

Buffy holds the phone, numb with shock.

                    GILES (O.C.)
      Buffy? Buffy, what is it?

Willow looks at Buffy, concerned. She grabs the phone out of her hand.

                    WILLOW
             (into phone)
      Thanks.

She hangs up. Buffy turns to Willow with resolve.

                    BUFFY
      I've got to get this thing, Willow.
      Before it gets those kids.

                    WILLOW
      You will. We will.

                    BUFFY
             (frustrated)
      But how? I can't even see it!

                    WILLOW
      You saw it once.

                    BUFFY
      Did I? Maybe my mind was playing
      with me. I mean, I was crazed with
      that fever and--

Buffy stops. She looks up at Willow.

                                                    CUT TO:

42 INT. DR. BACKER'S OFFICE - A MOMENT LATER (NIGHT)   42

Buffy reaches inside Dr. Backer's refrigerator and pulls out a RED-LABELED VIAL containing the virus.

                    WILLOW
      Buffy, think about this.

                                                    CONTINUED

42 CONTINUED: 42

                BUFFY
I am. Lots of thoughts

                WILLOW
It's crazy.

                BUFFY
The fever. That's how you see the Kindestod. That's why Celia could see it. That's why Ryan still can. It's the only way.

                WILLOW
But how can you fight this thing when you have a 107 degree temperature?

                BUFFY
I guess we'll find out.

Buffy raises the vial to her lips.

                WILLOW
Buffy!

                BUFFY
             (stopping)
Willow, I'm doing this--

                WILLOW
That's 100% pure. It'll kill you in an instant.

Buffy looks at the vial.

                BUFFY
They should put that on the label.

                WILLOW
             (sighs)
Here. It needs to be diluted.

She takes the vial, pours some water into a beaker and mixes a drop of the virus into it.

                BUFFY
This is going to have to work fast.

Willow puts another drop into the beaker.

                BUFFY (cont'd)
Faster than that.

                                        CONTINUED

42 CONTINUED: (2)   42

Willow pours in another drop and hands the beaker to Buffy.
Buffy looks at it; takes a breath.

                    BUFFY (cont'd)
        Here's to my health.

Buffy swallows it down.

43 INT. SUNNYDALE HOSPITAL CORRIDOR - LATER (NIGHT)   43

Buffy, who is starting to feel the effects of the virus, has
her arm over Willow's shoulder as they make their way to the
kids' ward.

                    BUFFY
        I'm not sure this was such a great
        idea.

                    WILLOW
        Hang in there. You'll be okay.

Buffy gets to the large window that looks into the kids'
ward. She steadies herself.

                    BUFFY
        Okay... I'm okay.

She TURNS to look through the window. Her face falls at what
she sees.

BUFFY'S POV: Through the window in the door.

Beds. Monitors. But no children.

Buffy stares through the window.

                    BUFFY (cont'd)
        They're gone.

                                                BLACK OUT.

                    END OF ACT THREE

ACT FOUR

44 INT. SUNNYDALE HOSPITAL BASEMENT - NIGHT   44

Ryan comes into view, with the rest of the kids trailing behind him. A few of the children COUGH and WHEEZE. The little girl struggles to keep up.

>   RYAN
>   Keep quiet!

Ryan goes to the little girl.

>   RYAN (cont'd)
>   It's not gonna find us here.

Ryan takes her by the hand and they continue on.

45 INT. SUNNYDALE HOSPITAL CORRIDOR - SAME TIME (NIGHT)   45

Buffy and Willow stand outside the kids' ward.

>   WILLOW
>   What could've happened?
>
>   BUFFY
>   (thinking)
>   I don't know. Maybe I'm too late.
>   Maybe they were moved. I don't want
>   to think about the other maybe.

Buffy SWAYS a bit and steadies herself on Willow.

>   BUFFY (cont'd)
>   Oh... I'm burning up.

Buffy puts her hand to her head and looks through the window again. She FREEZES.

>   BUFFY (cont'd)
>   Willow?
>
>   WILLOW
>   What?
>
>   BUFFY
>   I think it's in there.

BUFFY'S POV: through the window.

CONTINUED

45 CONTINUED: 45

A VAGUE SHAPE begins to SHIMMER into view, until the Kindestod is COMPLETELY VISIBLE to Buffy.

> BUFFY (cont'd)
> (through the window)
> Good to see you.

Buffy watches as the Kindestod SNIFFS around the room. He seems to have caught a scent.

Buffy goes to the door and tries to open it. It's LOCKED. The noise causes the Kindestod to look up. He SMILES. He turns away, keeps sniffing -- the scent takes him out through a door marked (you guessed it) "Basement Access."

> BUFFY (cont'd)
> He's going after them.

She RAMS her shoulder into the door, trying to break it down, but she's too weak. With all her might, she tries again. Nothing. She falls against the door.

> BUFFY (cont'd)
> We've got to get him.
> (then, wearily)
> Give me a second and we'll get him.

Dr. Wilkinson comes around a corner and sees the ill-looking Buffy leaning against the door. She goes to her.

> DR. WILKINSON
> Buffy, what's wrong?

> WILLOW
> She's... not feeling well. Again.

Dr. Wilkinson puts her arm around Buffy.

> DR. WILKINSON
> You should be in bed.

> BUFFY
> I'm fine. Really.

> DR. WILKINSON
> No. You're coming with me.

Buffy tries to pull away from her, but Dr. Wilkinson is insistent, almost dragging Buffy down the hall.

CONTINUED

45 CONTINUED: (2)   45

                    BUFFY
              No!

Buffy SHOVES Dr. Wilkinson away. She falls backwards, against a wall.

                    WILLOW
                (sympathetically; to
                 Dr. Wilkinson)
              She's sorry...

Buffy and Willow take off down the hall.

Dr. Wilkinson hurriedly reaches for a phone on the wall. Her words ECHO throughout the hospital.

                    DR. WILKINSON
                (into phone)
              Security to the children's ward. We
              have a situation. Security!

46 INT. SUNNYDALE HOSP. - ANOTHER CORRIDOR - A MOMENT LATER   46

Buffy and Willow come around a corner. Buffy stumbles a bit; Willow helps her along.

They look up and see Don and another SECURITY GUARD running towards them. The girls stop, trapped. Don slaps his billy club in his palm repeatedly.

                    DON
              Come on, now. Let's make this easy.

Buffy and Willow look at each other. Willow looks back at the guards. Then:

She goes crazy. She SCREAMS and fights off an invisible attack of:

                    WILLOW
              Bats! Arrghh! Get them off me!
              Horrible, horrible bats!

The guards head towards Willow. Buffy backs away.

She SLIPS AWAY as the security guards grab Willow. Dr. Wilkinson appears from the other direction.

                    DR. WILKINSON
              Not her. The other one!

                                                        CONTINUED

BUFFY THE VAMPIRE SLAYER "Killed By Death" (WHITE) 2/2/98   49.

46 CONTINUED: 46

Willow stops fighting, suddenly serene.

                    WILLOW
              No more bats.

The guards let go of her; look up and down the hallway. No more Buffy, either.

                                              CUT TO:

47 INT. SUNNYDALE HOSPITAL ENTRANCE AREA - NIGHT   47

Buffy STAGGERS into view. She stops, nearly winded. Bends over, hands on her knees, as she catches her breath.

Xander runs up, breathless and panicked.

                    XANDER
              Buffy! Are you okay? Did Angel get
              in?

                    BUFFY
              We have to get to the basement.

She staggers forward, her head heavy.

                    BUFFY (cont'd)
                  (weakly)
              Give me your... you.

She puts her arm over Xander's shoulder and they follow after the Kindestod.

48 INT. SUNNYDALE HOSPITAL BASEMENT - NIGHT   48

We PAN along the wall and find the kids HUDDLED together in a corner. The little girl SHIVERS and SHAKES.

                    RYAN
              Here.

Ryan takes off his jacket and wraps it around her. She looks up at him.

                    RYAN (cont'd)
              It's okay. We're going to be safe
              in--

Suddenly, the Kindestod is behind him. The kids SCREAM.

52

49 INT. SUNNYDALE HOSPITAL STAIRWELL - CONT. - NIGHT   49

Xander helps Buffy down quickly.

>   XANDER
>   You don't know how to kill this thing.
>
>   BUFFY
>   (grim determination)
>   I thought I might try violence.
>
>   XANDER
>   Solid call.

50 INT. SUNNYDALE HOSPITAL BASEMENT - CONT. - NIGHT   50

The Kindestod LIFTS Ryan into the air, then TOSSES him to the ground. The Kindestod JUMPS on top of Ryan and PINS his arms down. Ryan KICKS and tries to FIGHT HIM OFF.

The Kindestod's eyes BULGE, then begin to PROTRUDE from his head. They extend downward like tentacles and ATTACH themselves against Ryan's forehead, PRESSING IN hard. Ryan's struggles quickly subside as his strength is drained.

A two-by-four SMASHES into the Kindestod's face. He rolls backwards, off of Ryan, revealing BUFFY standing there. She glares at the Kindestod.

>   BUFFY
>   You make me sick.

The creature dives at Buffy and they begin to wrestle. Buffy is weak from the fever, but she gives it her all -- swinging, kicking, mostly missing.

Xander goes to Ryan and helps him up.

>   XANDER
>   Come on!

Xander herds him and the other kids to the door. Looking back he sees:

XANDER'S POV: Buffy fights nothing.

NEW ANGLE:

Buffy and the Kindestod (visible to us) continue their fight. Buffy JUMPS on his back. He FLIPS Buffy over, SNARLS, and pins her to the floor. Buffy struggles to free herself, but she's too weak. She's trapped.

                                                      CONTINUED

50 CONTINUED: 50

The Kindestod STARES down at her. His eyes BULGE OUT and begin extending down towards Buffy's forehead.

> BUFFY
> And the winner is...

With her last bit of strength, Buffy reaches up with both hands, grabs the Kindestod by the head, and TWISTS, cracking his neck.

> BUFFY (cont'd)
> Power Girl.

She dumps the body to the ground, standing up as Xander approaches.

> XANDER
> Are you okay?

> BUFFY
> Actually, I'm starting to feel better.

She wobbles, then COLLAPSES. Xander is there to catch her.

DISSOLVE TO:

51 INT. BUFFY'S BEDROOM - DAY (A FEW DAYS LATER) 51

Joyce comes in with a smile, carrying a tray of food -- sandwich, soup, juice, the works. She's clearly enjoying getting to play mother to her daughter.

> JOYCE
> Here you go, honey. Peanut butter and extra jelly. With the crust off, just the way you like it.

We MOVE with Joyce to REVEAL Buffy sitting upright in her bed (on top of the covers). She is flanked by Xander and Willow. All have made themselves comfortable, slouching against the headboard, watching TV with their shoes kicked off, drinking sodas, etc.

Joyce sets the tray in front of Buffy.

> BUFFY
> (pointing to a glass)
> And the juice?

CONTINUED

51 CONTINUED: 51

> JOYCE
> Two parts orange, one part grapefruit.

> BUFFY
> That's my drink.

> JOYCE
> I measured exactly.

Joyce starts to go--

> BUFFY (O.C.)
> Mom?

--then turns back. Buffy has lifted the top piece of bread from her sandwich.

> BUFFY
> (sheepishly)
> I wanted crunchy style.

> JOYCE
> Oh. I'm sorry.

She picks up the plate with a smile.

> BUFFY
> And, um, I ordered <u>extra</u> jelly.

> JOYCE
> Anything to help my daughter get well.

Willow rattles the ice in her glass.

> WILLOW
> While you're up, could I get a refill?

Joyce looks at her, the smile fading a bit.

> WILLOW (cont'd)
> It's just... I'm so comfortable.

> JOYCE
> (taking her glass)
> Of course.

> XANDER
> Ooh, and another bag of Chee-Zee Chips.

CONTINUED

51 CONTINUED: (2)   51

                        JOYCE
              You ate the last one.

                        XANDER
              No. I saw another bag hidden behind
              the raisins.

                        JOYCE
                    (gritting her teeth)
              I'm on it.

She starts out.

                        XANDER
                    (sotto, to Buffy)
              Your mom's trying to bogart the Chee-
              Zee Chips. What's <u>that</u> all about?

                        JOYCE
              Oh, Buffy. Here.

Joyce stops at the door and turns back, pulling an envelope out of her pocket.

                        JOYCE (cont'd)
              This came in the mail.

Buffy takes it; looks at the return address.

                        BUFFY
              It's from Ryan.

Buffy OPENS the letter and pulls out a piece of paper; looks at it. She SMILES. Joyce looks over Buffy's shoulder.

                        JOYCE
              Oh, he drew you a picture. Isn't
              that...

CLOSE-UP of the drawing -- Ryan's crayon rendition of Buffy ('Power Girl!' written on her shirt) standing triumphantly over the broken, horribly bloodied body of Der Kindestod. Rather grotesque.

                        JOYCE (O.C.)
                    (appalled)
              ...nice...

                                                    BLACK OUT.

                        END OF SHOW

Episode # 5V19
Story # 4973

BUFFY THE VAMPIRE SLAYER

"I Only Have Eyes For You"

Written By

Marti Noxon

Directed By

James Whitmore Jr.

SHOOTING SCRIPT

February 10, 1998 (WHITE)
February 12, 1998 (BLUE PAGES)
February 12, 1998 (PINK PAGES)

BUFFY THE VAMPIRE SLAYER "I Only Have Eyes For You" (BLUE) 2/12/98

BUFFY THE VAMPIRE SLAYER

"I Only Have Eyes For You"

CAST LIST

```
BUFFY SUMMERS......................... Sarah Michelle Gellar
XANDER HARRIS......................... Nicholas Brendon
RUPERT GILES.......................... Anthony S. Head
WILLOW ROSENBERG...................... Alyson Hannigan
CORDELIA CHASE........................ Charisma Carpenter
ANGEL................................. David Boreanaz

SPIKE.................................*James Marsters
DRUSILLA..............................*Juliet Landau
PRINCIPLE SNYDER......................*Armin Shimerman
JAMES................................. Chris Gorham
GRACE NEWMAN..........................*Meredith Salinger
MR. MILLER............................*James Lurie
JANITOR............................... John Hawkes
MISS FRANK............................*Miriam Flynn
FIGHTING BOY..........................*Brian Poth
FIGHTING GIRL.........................*Sarah Bibb
POLICE CHIEF..........................*Brian Reddy
BEN...................................*Ryan Teszareak
50'S GIRL #1..........................*Anna Coman-Hidy
50'S GIRL #2..........................*Vanessa Bednar

THE BAND..............................*Splendid
```

BUFFY THE VAMPIRE SLAYER "I Only Have Eyes For You" (BLUE) 2/12/98

BUFFY THE VAMPIRE SLAYER

"I Only Have Eyes For You"

SET LIST
=======

INTERIORS

SUNNYDALE HIGH SCHOOL
    HALLWAY
    ANOTHER PART OF THE HALLWAY
    SNYDER'S OFFICE
    COMPUTER CLASSROOM
    HISTORY CLASS
    LIBRARY
    GILES' OFFICE
    SCHOOL HALLWAY NEAR BALCONY
    GIRLS' BATHROOM
    CAFETERIA
   *STAIR LANDING - LOUNGE
    MUSIC ROOM
    HALL NEAR MUSIC ROOM
    HALL NEAR LIBRARY

BUFFY'S HOUSE
    BUFFY'S ROOM
    KITCHEN
    LIVING ROOM

BRONZE

EXTERIORS

SUNNYDALE HIGH SCHOOL
    BALCONY
    BOTTOM OF STAIRS NEAR BALCONY

NEW VAMPIRE LAIR
    GARDEN AREA

BUFFY THE VAMPIRE SLAYER

"I Only Have Eyes For You"

TEASER

1 INT. BRONZE - NIGHT   1

The place is packed. Couples slow dance as A BAND plays a
mellow, sexy song. BUFFY sits by herself, a little glum.

XANDER AND CORDY

Dance past. Enjoying an atypical moment of peace together.

ON WILLOW

Moving through the crowd with some drinks, she sees Buffy
looking bummed - wishes she could do something for her broken-
hearted friend. But her expression brightens when an
especially handsome, sweet-looking guy, BEN, approaches Buffy.

ON BUFFY AND CUTE GUY

                    BEN
          Hey. I'm Ben. We had Algebra II
          together last year.

Buffy searches   can't remember.

                    BUFFY
          Sorry. I pretty much repress
          anything math related.

                    BEN
          Miss Jackson. Second period. You
          were in the seat three over - one
          behind.

                    BUFFY
               (smiles)
          Oh - yeah... I remember now.
          Weren't there chalkboards and pencils
          and desks and stuff?

                    BEN
          That's the one!

                    BUFFY
               (taps her head)
          Like a steel trap.

                                                    CONTINUED

1   CONTINUED: 1

>   BEN
>   So... I was wondering... You know
>   that dance tomorrow night? Are you
>   going?
>
>   BUFFY
>   The Sadie Hawkins thing? Isn't that
>   the deal where the girls ask the boys?
>
>   BEN
>   Yeah. And I thought, maybe, if
>   you're free you might... ask me.

Buffy balks. Her discomfort is obvious.

>   BUFFY
>   Oh... Gosh... I-

Ben sees where this is going - tries to save face.

>   BEN
>   Hey. No. Don't worry about it.
>
>   BUFFY
>   It's not you. You seem great. It's
>   just - I'm not seeing anybody. Ever
>   again, actually.
>
>   BEN
>   Oh. That's too bad. Okay. Well.
>   I'd better...
>
>   ON WILLOW

Watching as BEN walks away from Buffy - rejected. Buffy grabs her purse and starts for the door. Willow moves quickly - heads Buffy off at the pass before she can leave.

>   WILLOW
>   Hey. You bailing?
>
>   BUFFY
>   Yeah. I'm gonna stop by the library
>   and see if Giles wants me to patrol.
>   Then sack it.
>
>   WILLOW
>   You've been doing a lot of that.
>   Patrolling and sacking. In fact,
>   you've kinda been all work, no play
>   Buffy.

CONTINUED

BUFFY THE VAMPIRE SLAYER "I Only Have Eyes For You" (WHITE) 2/10/98   3.

1   CONTINUED: (2)   1

                        BUFFY
              I play. I have big fun. I came here
              tonight, didn't I?

                        WILLOW
              You came. You saw. You rejected.

                        BUFFY
              You mean that guy? I'm... just not
              in date-mode right now.

                        WILLOW
              But maybe you need to date to get in
              date mode.

                        BUFFY
              But I don't think I'm ready.

                        WILLOW
              You're thinking too much. Maybe you
              should just be impulsive!

                        BUFFY
              Impulsive. Do you remember my ex-
              boyfriend, the vampire? I slept with
              him. He lost his soul. My boyfriend
              is gone forever and the demon that is
              wearing his face is killing my
              friends. The next impulsive decision
              I make will involve my choice of
              <u>dentures</u>.

                        WILLOW
              Okay, the Angel thing went badly, I'm
              on board with that. But that's not
              your fault.
                   (off Buffy's look)
              And anyways, love isn't always like
              that. Love can be... nice.

                                        SMASH CUT TO:

2   INT. SCHOOL HALLWAY - NIGHT   2

    A teenage couple rounds a corner in the dark hallway, which
    is decorated WITH BANNERS ANNOUNCING THE UPCOMING SADIE
    HAWKINS DANCE. The kids are in the middle of a horrible,
    emotional argument - like they're fighting for their lives.

                        FIGHTING BOY
              Come back here! We're not finished!

                                              CONTINUED

BUFFY THE VAMPIRE SLAYER "I Only Have Eyes For You" (WHITE) 2/10/98 4.

2 CONTINUED: 2

The boy grabs her arm. Stops her.

                  FIGHTING BOY (cont'd)
     You don't care anymore? Is that it?

                  FIGHTING GIRL
     It doesn't matter. It doesn't matter
     what I feel-

                  FIGHTING BOY
     Then tell me you don't love me.

She's silent. He burns. Shakes her - hard. Yells.

                  FIGHTING BOY (cont'd)
     Say it!

The girl starts to cry.

                  FIGHTING GIRL
     Will that help? Is that what you
     have to hear?
         (lying)
     I don't. I don't. Now let me go!

She struggles to break his grasp - but he holds on.
Devastated - disbelieving.

                  FIGHTING BOY
     No... A person doesn't just wake up
     one day and stop loving somebody.

Now he RAISES the GUN he's been holding so she can see it.
His rage and fear pushing him to the edge. Her eyes widen in
horror.

                  FIGHTING BOY (cont'd)
     Love is forever.

                                            BLACK OUT.

                    END OF TEASER

ACT ONE

3   INT. SCHOOL HALLWAY - NIGHT   3

The COUPLE FROM THE TEASER are still at it. The girl struggles in the boy's grasp as he holds the GUN closer to her, shaking with emotion.

                    FIGHTING BOY
          I'm not afraid to use it. I swear.
          If I can't be with you-

                    FIGHTING GIRL
          Oh my God-

BUFFY enters the hallway - sees the couple as the girl manages to SHOVE the boy away and head for an EXIT that leads to a balcony.

                    FIGHTING GIRL (cont'd)
          No! Please!-

The boy scrambles after her - raises the GUN as if he might fire.

                    FIGHTING BOY
          Don't walk away from me, bitch!-

Buffy reacts - runs to stop him.

                    BUFFY
          Hey! Leave her alone!

4   INT. ANOTHER PART OF THE HALLWAY - CONT. (NIGHT)   4

We see a JANITOR moving down another hallway. He hears the commotion and comes running.

5   INT. SCHOOL HALLWAY - CONT. (NIGHT)   5

The janitor rounds the corner just as BUFFY GRABS the boy. They struggle briefly before she KNOCKS THE GUN FROM HIS HAND. It SKITTERS down the hall and out of sight.

Buffy wrestles the boy to the ground. The Janitor moves to the crying girl. The BOY BLINKS. Suddenly power-freaked.

                    FIGHTING BOY
          It's... What happened?

                                                              CONTINUED

BUFFY THE VAMPIRE SLAYER "I Only Have Eyes For You" (WHITE) 2/10/98 6.

5 CONTINUED: 5

                    BUFFY
          What happened? You went OJ on your
          girlfriend!

                    FIGHTING BOY
                 (desperate/baffled)
          This is nuts... I don't know why
          I - I got so mad...

                    BUFFY
          Because you're a jerk?

Now the girl speaks up. She also looks totally freaked.

                    FIGHTING GIRL
          He's not. We weren't even fighting
          a few minutes ago.

                    FIGHTING BOY
          We weren't. I swear to God...

                    BUFFY
          If you weren't fighting - why did you
          have a gun?

                    FIGHTING BOY
          I don't know. I - I don't even know
          where I got it.

THE JANITOR is scanning the floor. Shrugs.

                    JANITOR
          I don't see any gun.

Off Buffy - at a loss.

6 INT. SNYDER'S OFFICE - DAY   6

Buffy sits in the "hot seat" while Snyder, worked up, grills
her.

                    SNYDER
          I'm sure you know why I asked you
          here.

                    BUFFY
                 (weakly hopeful)
          To thank me?

                                                            CONTINUED

6 CONTINUED: 6

                    SNYDER
          That's right. I want to thank you.
          What would Sunnydale High do without
          you around to incite mayhem, chaos
          and disorder?

                    BUFFY
          What? I didn't incite! I stopped
          that boy from killing his girlfriend.
          I mean - ask them. Ask the janitor-

                    SNYDER
          People can be coerced, Summers. I'm
          no stranger to conspiracy. I saw JFK.
                    (then)
          I'm a truth seeker. I've got a
          missing gun and two confused kids on
          my hands. Pieces of a puzzle. I'm
          going to look at all those pieces
          carefully and rationally. And I'm
          going to keep looking until I figure
          out exactly how this is all your
          fault.

He'd go on but his intercom buzzes.

                    VOICE ON INTERCOM (O.C.)
          Mr. Snyder? Billy Crandle chained
          himself to the snack machine again.

Snyder shakes his head - fuming. Starts for the door.

                    SNYDER
          Pathetic little no-life vegan.

Buffy starts to get up but SNYDER pushes her back into her chair.

                    SNYDER (cont'd)
          Not so fast, Missy. I'm not done
          with you yet. You stink of lies.

He leaves.

CLOSE ON BOOK SHELF

Where Snyder's YEARBOOK COLLECTION is. Unseen by Buffy, one of the yearbooks is drawn out BY AN INVISIBLE FORCE. It falls to the ground with a thud.

ON BUFFY

                                                              CONTINUED

BUFFY THE VAMPIRE SLAYER "I Only Have Eyes For You" (WHITE) 2/10/98   8.

6   CONTINUED: (2)   6

Startled by the book falling. She rises and picks it up - looks at the cover.

CLOSE ON YEARBOOK

It's from 1955.

ON BUFFY

Only mildly curious as she puts it back on the shelf.

7   EXT. SCHOOL - DAY   7

Xander and Cordelia walk together on their way to class.

> CORDELIA
> Okay. So what's up with Buffy?

> XANDER
> How many times do we have to go over this? Nothing's up with Buffy. We're just good friends-

> CORDELIA
> No, I mean, what's up with **Buffy**? Like, is she okay?

> XANDER
> Sorry. I'm not used to you addressing subjects not directly related to... you.
> (then)
> She's fine. I guess. Why?

> CORDELIA
> She only blew off Ben Straley - the most eligible hunk in town. He's totally rad and his father owns a **department store**. I mean, he's the guy I'd be going out with if I wasn't so obviously brain damaged. No offense.

> XANDER
> Oh no. Why would I be offended?

> CORDELIA
> Anyway. Ben told Lynette who told Charity - that Buffy wouldn't even give him the time of day.

CONTINUED

BUFFY THE VAMPIRE SLAYER "I Only Have Eyes For You" (WHITE) 2/10/98 9.

7   CONTINUED: 7

                    XANDER
          Good for her. She's providing much
          needed life experience for the
          rejection-deprived.

                    CORDELIA
          The guilt thing's just getting a
          little old, you know. Everybody's
          told her what happened to Angel isn't
          her fault.

                    XANDER
          Yeah. Everybody except the one guy
          she needs to hear it from.

8   INT. COMPUTER CLASSROOM - DAY   8

    GILES comes to the doorway. Unnoticed, he watches Willow,
    who is still teaching as Calendar's temporary replacement.

                    WILLOW
          So for next time, read the chapters
          on information groupings and binary
          coding. I bet you'll think coding is
          pretty cool - I mean, if you find two
          digit multi-stacked conversions and
          primary number clusters a big hoot.

    The class LAUGHS APPRECIATIVELY at her computer geek joke as
    the bell rings.

    ON GILES

    Clearly lost. If there was a joke - he missed it.

    WILLOW

    Sees him as the students file out.

                    WILLOW (cont'd)
                        (excited)
          Giles. I made them laugh, did you
          hear? I did the joke thing!

                    GILES
          Yes. So it seems. I mean - you did.
          Good show.
                        (then)
          I was dropping by see if you needed
          assistance - but you appear to have
          things quite under control.

                                                        CONTINUED

BUFFY THE VAMPIRE SLAYER "I Only Have Eyes For You" (WHITE) 2/10/98 10.

8 CONTINUED: 8

> WILLOW
> Well, I had really good lesson plans.
> Ms. Calendar had them on her computer.

A shadow crosses Giles' features. It's not lost on Willow - who treads gently.

> GILES
> Yes, she was... dedicated, wasn't she?

> WILLOW
> I also found a bunch of files and internet sights about paganism and majik and stuff.

> GILES
> Oh?

> WILLOW
> Yeah, it's really interesting...

Willow moves to the desk. Finds a small pink stone on a black silk cord, which she hands to him.

> WILLOW (cont'd)
> And - this was in her drawer. She told me it's rose quartz - that it has healing powers.
> (then)
> I thought she'd want you to have it.

ON GILES

Who closes his hand around the stone - touched, distraught.

> GILES
> Thank you, Willow. That's very thoughtful of you.

9 INT. HISTORY CLASS - DAY 9

Buffy's in HISTORY CLASS. The teacher, MR. MILLER, stands at the chalk board, writing away and talking in a colorless monotone-

> MR. MILLER
> ...before 1935 the New Deal focused on revitalizing stricken business and agricultural communities...

The WHOLE CLASS IS BORED BEYOND BELIEF. Many of them can barely keep their eyes open.

CONTINUED

BUFFY THE VAMPIRE SLAYER "I Only Have Eyes For You" (WHITE) 2/10/98 11.

9   CONTINUED: 9

   MOVE IN ON BUFFY

   As she fights sleep. But Miller's voice is like white noise.

                    MR. MILLER (O.C.)
              The New Deal also tried to regulate
              the nation's financial hierarchy-

   Finally - her EYELIDS droop and CLOSE.

10 INT. HISTORY CLASS - BUFFY'S DREAM - CIRCA 1955 - DAY   10

   FROM BUFFY'S POV

   Buffy is in the same classroom, but it's obvious from the
   decor and clothes that she's dreaming about THE 50'S. Class
   has just ended. A couple of cute girls giggle as they look
   at a flyer for the 1955 SADIE HAWKINS DANCE.

                    50'S GIRL #1
              I told Mrs. Hall we'd go help
              decorate the gym. Who are you taking?

                    50'S GIRL #2
              David said yes.

                    50'S GIRL #1
              You're kidding! He's so dreamy.

   They MOVE OFF as Buffy nears the TEACHER'S DESK. Sees a
   beautiful young teacher, GRACE NEWMAN, who smiles kindly as
   she takes papers. The kids file out, except for JAMES, who
   lingers. He's big, handsome - not at all boyish. He hands
   Miss Newman his paper-

   CLOSE ON THEIR HANDS

   Which TOUCH as she takes the paper from him.

   BACK ON JAMES AND MISS NEWMAN

   There is obvious heat between them. It flusters Miss Newman.

                    MISS NEWMAN
              Thank you, James.
                    (then)
              How are you enjoying that book I
              loaned you? The Hemmingway?

                    JAMES
              I like it. Very much.

                                                              CONTINUED

                                   70

10 CONTINUED: 10

> Impulsively, he touches her hand again. He moves closer.
> They both know they shouldn't be talking like this.

                        JAMES (cont'd)
        It's honest.

They lock eyes. Miss Newman stammers-

                        GRACE NEWMAN
        I - Yes. It's based on a true
        story, actually. He fell in love
        with his-

She stops as his hand moves up her arm. They move closer, eyes on each other. They're interrupted as the door to the classroom starts to open. JAMES AND MISS NEWMAN pull quickly apart, startled.

11 INT. HISTORY CLASS - DAY   11

ON BUFFY

Who wakes, also startled. She looks around, disoriented - sees that she's back in the present day. At the board, MR. MILLER is still writing and tediously narrating.

                        MR. MILLER
        ...to revive industrial activity, the
        NRA, the National Recovery
        Administration...

He turns away from the board to look at the class, but continues to write. As he's talking his hand starts to scrawl in LARGE ANGRY LETTERS - "DON'T WALK AWAY FROM ME, BITCH." Mr. Miller doesn't even notice what he's doing. Keeps talking-

                      MR. MILLER (cont'd)
        ...assigned a number of task forces-

The class REACTS WITH SHOCK and Mr. Miller looks back at the board. He's clearly confused and embarrassed by what he's just written.

                      MR. MILLER (cont'd)
        Oh! Good God.

He immediately ERASES the phrase.

ON BUFFY

Stunned.

BUFFY THE VAMPIRE SLAYER "I Only Have Eyes For You" (WHITE) 2/10/98 13.

12 INT. SCHOOL HALLWAY - DAY   12

Buffy is walking with Xander.

      BUFFY
  I'm telling you, something weird is
  going on.

      XANDER
  Something weird is going on. Isn't
  that our school motto?

      BUFFY
  Pretty much. But this time... I
  don't know. It bugs me.

They arrive at Xander's locker, which he does the combo on.

      XANDER
  I'm not trying to poo poo your
  wiggins, but a domestic dispute and
  a little case of chalkboard
  Tourette's? Sounds like "Hellmouth
  Lite" to me-

Xander opens his locker and A BLUE, DECAYING ARM BURSTS from
inside and GRABS HIM BY THE SHIRT. Xander, of course,
screams for real this time. The ARM starts to PULL XANDER
INTO THE LOCKER. After a brief struggle, Buffy manages to
rip Xander's shirt and free him of the death grip. She SLAMS
the LOCKER SHUT.

A horrified beat as they both stare at the locker. Then
Buffy FLINGS the locker door open again - ready to fight.
But - to their surprise - there's nothing. They look inside.

CLOSE ON LOCKER

Except for Xander's stuff - it's empty.

13 INT. LIBRARY - DAY   13

Willow is studying while Giles goes about some researchy
stuffy of some kind. Now XANDER and BUFFY enter, tripping.
Xander looks a mess - what with his ripped shirt and all.

      WILLOW
  Xander. What did you do - criticize
  Cordelia's outfit?

      XANDER
  You're just a big bucket o' funny,
  Will.
     (more)

                CONTINUED

13 CONTINUED: 13

> XANDER (cont'd)
> I'll have you know I just got accosted by some kind of locker monster.
>
> GILES
> (perks up)
> Loch Ness monster? Really?
>
> BUFFY
> Locker monster. Is what he said. But it wasn't really a "monster". It was more like a guy reached out and grabbed him. But when we opened the locker a second time - gone. Nothing.
>
> XANDER
> This is right after Buffy's history teacher started doing some freaky channeling thing in class.
>
> GILES
> Fascinating. It sounds like paranormal phenomena.
>
> WILLOW
> A ghost? Cool!
>
> XANDER
> Oh no, not cool. This was no wimpy chain-rattler. This was more - "I'm dead as hell and I'm not gonna take it anymore."
>
> GILES
> Exactly. Despite the Xander-speak, that's an accurate definition of a poltergeist.
>
> XANDER
> I defined something? Accurately? Check me out.
> (he slams a book on
> the table shut)
> Guess I'm done with the book learning!
>
> BUFFY
> So we've got some bad boo on our hands?

CONTINUED

13 CONTINUED: (2)   13

                    GILES
          Well... A poltergeist is extremely
          disruptive - and what you described
          certainly fits the bill.

                    WILLOW
          But why is it here? Does it just
          want to scare people?

                    GILES
          It doesn't know exactly what it
          wants. That's the problem. Many
          times the spirit is plagued by all
          manner of worldly troubles. But,
          being dead, it has no way to make
          it's peace. So it lashes out.
          Growing ever more confused, ever more
          angry...

                    BUFFY
          So - it's like a regular teenager.
          Only dead.

                    WILLOW
          What can we do? Is there any way to
          stop it?

                    GILES
          The only tried and true way is to
          figure out what unresolved issues
          keep the spirit here - and resolve
          them.

                    BUFFY
          Great. So now we're Dr. Laura for
          the deceased.

                    GILES
          Only if we can find out who this
          spirit is. Or... was.

     He stops, something occurring to him. Perhaps he knows who
     it is?

14   INT. SCHOOL HALLWAY - NIGHT   14

     It's late. The hallway is mostly dark as THE JANITOR mops
     the floor - humming to himself. Now a TEACHER - MISS
     FRANK - steps out of her classroom with her briefcase and
     heads for the exit. They smile politely.

                                                        CONTINUED

14 CONTINUED: 14

                    JANITOR
          Working late, Miss Frank?

                    MISS FRANK
          It's my fault. Let myself get behind.
                    (looks at floor)
          Is it okay to walk here, George? It
          is... George, right?

                    JANITOR
          Yes, ma'am. You go ahead.

                    MISS FRANK
          Thanks. You have a nice evening.

                    JANITOR
          You too. Drive safe.

He goes back to his mopping and she starts to walk away. But
the janitor pauses. Looks back at Miss Frank.

                    JANITOR (cont'd)
          Oh, Miss Frank?

She stops. Turns.

                    MISS FRANK
          Yes?

Something shifts in his eyes. They go cold - full of rage.

                    JANITOR
          You can't make me disappear just
          because you say it's over.

                    MISS FRANK
          There's no way we can be together.
          No way people will ever understand,
          accept it-

                    JANITOR
          Is that what this is about? What
          other people think?

                    MISS FRANK
                    (emphatic)
          No! I just want you to be able to
          have some kind of normal life. We
          can never have that - don't you see?

                                                              CONTINUED

14 CONTINUED: (2)   14

                    JANITOR
          I don't give a damn about a normal
          life.
                    (pleading)
          I'm going crazy, not seeing you. I
          think about you every minute-

She obviously feels the same way. Pushes it down.

                    MISS FRANK
          I know. But...
                    (then)
          It's over. It has to be.

She starts to walk away from him. Which PROVOKES his anger
and hurt even more. He shouts-

                    JANITOR
          Come back here! We're not finished!

He grabs her arm. Stops her.

                    JANITOR (cont'd)
          You don't care anymore? Is that it?

                    MISS FRANK
          It doesn't matter. It doesn't matter
          what I feel-

                    JANITOR
          Then tell me you don't love me.

She's silent. He burns. Shakes her - hard.

                    JANITOR (cont'd)
          Say it!

Miss Frank starts to cry.

                    MISS FRANK
          Will that help? Is that what you
          have to hear?
                    (lying)
          I don't. I don't. Now let me go!

She struggles to break his grasp - but he holds on.
Devastated - disbelieving.

                    JANITOR
          No... A person doesn't just wake up
          one day and stop loving somebody.

ANGLE: In the janitor's empty hand, a gun magically appears.

                                                        CONTINUED

BUFFY THE VAMPIRE SLAYER "I Only Have Eyes For You" (WHITE) 2/10/98 18.

14 CONTINUED: (3)   **14**

Now he RASIES the GUN so she can see it. His rage and fear pushing him to the edge. Her eyes widen with horror.

                         JANITOR (cont'd)
Love is forever.

                                                    BLACK OUT.

                         END OF ACT ONE

BUFFY THE VAMPIRE SLAYER "I Only Have Eyes For You" (WHITE) 2/10/98 19.

ACT TWO

15 INT. LIBRARY - NIGHT   15

All is quiet in the library as Giles works late again. A number of books on GHOSTS and COMMUNICATING WITH THE DEAD are open before him. As he reads, he unconsciously rolls Jenny's rose quartz stone around in his hand.

Now a whispery voice rises from the silence. A woman.

                    WOMAN'S VOICE (O.C.)
              ...I need you...

Giles looks up - startled. He contemplates the empty room.

                    GILES
                  (hopeful)
              Jenny?

He stands and starts toward the doors of the library.

16 INT. SCHOOL HALLWAY NEAR BALCONY - NIGHT   16

Giles moves tentatively into hallway - now hears a muffled argument. Through the windows in the doors at the end of the hallway, he can see the JANITOR yelling at MISS FRANK outside on the balcony.

17 EXT. BALCONY - CONT. (NIGHT)   17

The janitor still has the gun, which shakes wildly in his hand as he rages.

                    MISS FRANK
                  (carefully)
              Let's both... just calm down. Give
              me the gun.

                    JANITOR
              Don't! Don't do that, damn it!

CLOSE ON MISS FRANK

Reacting to his venom as he continues.

                    JANITOR (O.C.)
              Don't talk to me like I'm some dumb-

BOOM! The gun discharges.

78

BUFFY THE VAMPIRE SLAYER "I Only Have Eyes For You" (WHITE) 2/10/98 20.

18 INT. SCHOOL HALLWAY NEAR BALCONY - NIGHT   18

Giles, on his way to the balcony to stop the fight, FLINCHES at the sound of the gun.

19 EXT. BALCONY - NIGHT   19

Miss Frank looks down at the gunshot wound in her chest - disbelieving - then FALLS back over the balcony and lands in a CRUMPLED HEAP ON THE STAIRS.

ON THE JANITOR

Panicked - he turns and RUNS back into the school

20 INT. SCHOOL HALLWAY NEAR BALCONY - NIGHT   20

The JANITOR races down the hallway. Giles surges forward and TACKLES the JANITOR. They struggle. As before, the gun is knocked out of the janitor's hands.

CLOSE ON GUN

As it comes to rest and MAGICALLY DISAPPEARS.

ON GILES AND JANITOR

Who are too involved in battle to notice this. Giles finally subdues the janitor with a HARD RIGHT HOOK. A stunned beat as the janitor quiets. Then-

                    JANITOR
      What - what's going on?

                    GILES
                  (aghast)
      What's going on? You just **shot** a
      woman...

OFF the janitor's confused, desperate face.

21 EXT. GARDEN AREA OF THE NEW VAMPIRE LAIR - NIGHT   21

Angel leads Drusilla out of an impressive art deco style house into a WALLED COURTYARD which is home to a LUSH, OVERGROWN GARDEN. A set of stairs in one corner leads to a street exit.

                    ANGEL
      ...and this - is the garden.

                                            CONTINUED

BUFFY THE VAMPIRE SLAYER "I Only Have Eyes For You" (WHITE) 2/10/98 21.

21 CONTINUED: 21

            Drusilla takes in the beautiful surroundings - thrilled.
            Moves to a WALL COVERED IN JASMINE.

                              DRUSILLA
                    Look. Jasmine.

            Angel goes to her - wraps his arms around her.

                              ANGEL
                    Night blooming.

                              DRUSILLA
                    Like us.
                         (gleeful)
                    Oooooh Angel, it's fairy-land!

            Now SPIKE wheels out of the house and into the yard. A beat
            as he takes in Dru and Angel's overly-friendly position.

                              SPIKE
                    It's paradise! Big windows and
                    lovely gardens. They'll be perfect
                    when we want the sunlight to <u>kill</u> <u>us</u>.

                              ANGEL
                    You don't like it, Spike? Hit the
                    stairs and go. Take a stand, man.

            Spike takes the dig - fuming.

                              SPIKE
                    Our old place was just fine. Until
                    you went and had us burned out.

                              ANGEL
                    Things change, Spiky. You've got to
                    roll with the punches... Well,
                    actually, you've pretty much got that
                    part down - haven't you?

            Once more, Spike takes it on the chin.

                              SPIKE
                    Very funny, mate.

                              ANGEL
                    What can I say?

            Angel grabs Drusilla again. Nuzzles her neck and leers at
            Spike - relishing his torment.

                              ANGEL (cont'd)
                    I just love to see you smile, buddy.

                                                              CONTINUED

21 CONTINUED: (2)   21

    ON SPIKE

Whose eyes BURN with rage. But he holds it together.

                    SPIKE
        Yeah. You're a giver.

22 INT. LIBRARY - DAY   22

    Buffy, Willow and Xander hang with Giles.

                    GILES
        It was just like with this couple you
        encountered the other night, Buffy.
        The janitor remembered everything.
        He knew he'd killed this poor
        woman - but he had no idea why. They
        had no intimate relationship.

                    WILLOW
        And the gun? Did you ever find it?

                    GILES
        No. The police, everybody... We
        looked all over.
            (then)
        I think it's very clear. What's
        happening.

                    XANDER
        Fill me in, then. 'Cause I've read
        the book, seen the movie and I'm
        still fuzzy about what's going on.

                    GILES
        It's Jenny.

                    BUFFY
        What?

                    XANDER
        You think she's the poltergeist?

                    GILES
        Don't you see? She died here under
        tragic conditions. Now she's trapped.

                    WILLOW
        But - what about the whole deal with
        the gun?
            (more)

                                                                                CONTINUED

22 CONTINUED: 22

>   WILLOW (cont'd)
>   (she glances at
>   Buffy, lowering her
>   voice)
>   Angel didn't shoot Ms. Calendar.

Buffy still registers the comment, looks down.

>   GILES
>   The gun is insignificant. It's the
>   violence of the thing that matters.

>   BUFFY
>   I don't know. It seems like the
>   fight these couples keep having is
>   sort of... specific. You know?

>   WILLOW
>   She's right, Giles. The gun, the
>   place... It's like a pattern that
>   doesn't fit with the way Ms. Calendar
>   died.

>   GILES
>   Yes. Well. I appreciate your
>   thoughts on the matter. In fact, I
>   encourage you to always challenge me
>   when you feel it's appropriate. You
>   must never be cowed by authority.
>   (quickly)
>   Except, of course, in this instance
>   when I am clearly **right** and you are
>   clearly **wrong.**

A beat. Then-

>   BUFFY
>   Great. Glad to know we have this
>   open line of communication.

23 INT. COMPUTER CLASSROOM - DAY 23

Not surprisingly - Buffy, Xander and Willow are now hanging without Giles.

>   WILLOW
>   This is freaky. I don't think I've
>   ever seen Giles be so pig-headed.

CONTINUED

23 CONTINUED: 23

> XANDER
> I know. He's usually "Investigate Things From Every Boring Angle" guy. Now he's "I Cling To My One Lame Idea" guy. What gives?

> BUFFY
> He misses her. He can't think. Just a little more fallout from my love life.

Willow moves to her computer. Starts with the clickity clack.

> WILLOW
> Okay, but this ghost stuff is something else. Let me do a cross check, look for other shootings at the school.

> BUFFY
> Yeah, we need some alternate ghost theories. What do we know?

> XANDER
> Dog spit is cleaner than human's.

> BUFFY
> Besides that.

Willow taps some keys. A moment as some information comes up on the screen. Then her expression registers shock.

> WILLOW
> Oh boy. We know plenty... It says here that a student murdered a teacher on the night of the Sadie Hawkins dance. The rumor was that they were having an affair and she tried to break it off. After he killed her, he went into the music room and shot himself.

As she relates the tale we see <u>FLASHBACKS</u> of the salient events. Finally:

> XANDER
> Ladies and gentlemen - we have a poltergeist. It has to be one of those two, right?

> WILLOW
> It all fits. The gun. The Sadie Hawkins dance...

CONTINUED

23 CONTINUED: (2) 23

                    BUFFY
          Which is **tonight**.

She stops, thinking.

                    XANDER
          How come we never heard about this
          murder/suicide thing before? When
          did it happen?

                    WILLOW
          Well, it says --

                    BUFFY
                (cutting her off)
          1955.

                    WILLOW
          How did you know?

24 INT. COMPUTER CLASSROOM - A LITTLE WHILE LATER (DAY)   24

CLOSE ON

A 1955 YEARBOOK HITS the desk. Willow opens it to an "In Memoriam" page for GRACE NEWMAN.

ON WILLOW, XANDER and BUFFY

                    BUFFY
          Okay. Fresh new strangeness? I
          dreamt about this woman the other
          day. Her and this young guy-

Willow turns some pages. Finds a photo of JAMES STANLEY.

                    WILLOW
          James Stanley?
                (off Buffy's nod)
          He's the one. He did it.

                    XANDER
          Your dreams are getting wicked
          accurate, Buff. You wouldn't happen
          to see me coming into big cash or,
          possibly, knowing the love of a
          woman? In a full-body sense?

                                              CONTINUED

24 CONTINUED: 24

                         BUFFY
                   (ignoring/still
                   looking at photo)
              He couldn't make her love him, so he
              killed her. What a sicko.

                         WILLOW
              He looks so normal in his picture.
              He was smart, too. He made the honor
              role.

                         BUFFY
              Smart?

                         XANDER
              He killed a person and he killed
              himself. Those are pretty much the
              two dumbest things you can do.

                         WILLOW
              I know, but... don't you feel kind of
              bad for them?

                         BUFFY
              I feel lousy. For her. He's a
              murderer. He should pay for it.

                         WILLOW
              With his life?

                         BUFFY
              No, he should be in prison for sixty
              years breaking rocks and making
              'special friends' with Roscoe the
              weight lifter.

Willow and Xander exchange a look. Buffy's vitriol is just
a bit too intense.

                         XANDER
              Yikes. The quality of mercy is **not**
              Buffy.

                         WILLOW
              Whose ghost do you think we're
              dealing with? His or hers?

                         BUFFY
              Considering how violent it is, I'd
              say it's his.

                         XANDER
              That tracks.

                                                              CONTINUED

24 CONTINUED: (2) 24

> WILLOW
> I've been browsing in some of Ms. Calendar's pagan sites. Maybe I can find a way to communicate with him. Find out what he wants.
>
> BUFFY
> Who cares what he wants? We gotta shut him down before some other innocent guy shoots some nice girl and blows his brains all over the music room wall.

Beat.

> XANDER
> Okay, who's hungry?

24 INT. CAFETERIA - DAY   25

The place is crowded with students as Xander sits with Willow and Buffy at a table. None of them are really enthused about their food.

Now CORDELIA comes over and sits next to Xander with a plate of spaghetti. She addresses them all, indignant.

                    CORDELIA
          I hope you guys weren't planning on
          going to this Sadie Hawkins dance
          tonight - because I'm totally
          organizing a boycott. Do you realize
          that the girls are supposed to ask
          the guys - and pay and everything?
          I mean, who's genius idea was that?

                    XANDER
          Obviously some hairy-legged feminist.

                    CORDELIA
          Really. We have to nip this in the
          bud or things could get way scary-

Speaking of - she's interrupted by a HORRIBLE YELL.

CLOSE ON

A guy at the table across from them. The sandwich he just bit into has turned into WRITHING BLACK SNAKES.

ON XANDER

Who looks down at his NACHO STICKS in terror. SNAKES.

THE WHOLE CAFETERIA

Erupts into total CHAOS. Everybody's food has transformed into WRIGGLING SERPENTS.

BUFFY

Does what she can. She YANKS a snake off a girl nearly FROZEN WITH FEAR.

ON THE DOORWAY TO THE CAFETERIA

Where SNYDER takes in MAYHEM. He is concerned but calm.

ON CORDELIA

Who SCREAMS at her SNAKE FILLED PLATE. She tries to toss it away from her, but one of the snakes COILS AND STRIKES - biting her on the FACE.

BUFFY THE VAMPIRE SLAYER "I Only Have Eyes For You" (WHITE) 2/10/98 28.

26 EXT. SCHOOL - DAY   26

The school is being evacuated. Exterminators move in as freaked students file out.

CLOSE ON CORDY

Who is having her face bandaged by a PARAMEDIC while XANDER holds her hand.

                CORDELIA
      Perfect. I'm going to be swollen and
      scarred. Why didn't it just kill me?

ON SNYDER AND THE POLICE CHIEF

Who speak cryptically.

                POLICE CHIEF
      School boy prank?

                SNYDER
        (shakes his head)
      Never sell.

                POLICE CHIEF
      Backed up sewer lines?

                SNYDER
      Better... I can probably make that
      one fly. But this is getting out of
      hand. People will talk.

                POLICE CHIEF
      You'll take care of it.

                SNYDER
      I'm doing everything I can. But you
      people have to realize that --
        (as people pass)
      -- backed up sewer line, this
      happened in San Diego just last
      week --
        (they're gone)
      -- that we are on a Hellmouth.
      Sooner or later, people are going to
      figure that out.

                POLICE CHIEF
      The city council was told you could
      handle this job. If you feel you
      can't... perhaps you'd like to take
      that up... with the Mayor.

Dread flushes Snyder's face.

                                            CONTINUED

BUFFY THE VAMPIRE SLAYER "I Only Have Eyes For You" (WHITE) 2/10/98 29.

26 CONTINUED: 26

    SNYDER
  I'll handle it. I will.

27 INT. BUFFY'S ROOM - NIGHT 27 *

Xander, Willow, Cordelia (still bandaged from the snake trauma) and Buffy are gathered.

    WILLOW
  Remember the plan to contact the
  spirit and talk to it? Scrap that
  plan.

Willow lays out a MAP OF THE SCHOOL that she's drawn.

    WILLOW (cont'd)
  Buffy, you're right. The time for
  touchy-feely communication has
  passed. I've done some homework and
  learned that the only solution - is
  the final solution.

    XANDER
  Nuke the school? I like it!

    WILLOW
  Not quite. Exorcism.

    CORDELIA
  Are you crazy? I saw that movie.
  Even the priests died!

    BUFFY
  What's the deal, Will?

Willow explains - using the map to make her point.

    WILLOW
  Okay. See here? The balcony?
  That's where the original teacher was
  shot back in 1955 and where Miss
  Frank died. It's the **hot spot** where
  all the bad mojo is coming from. We
  need to create a Mangus Tripod-
    (draws on map)
  One person chants here, in the hot
  spot, and the other three people
  chant in other areas of the school -
  making a triangle. It's supposed to
  bind the bad spirit. Stop it from
  doing more harm.

CONTINUED

27 CONTINUED: 27

> BUFFY
> I'll take the hot spot. If there's real trouble, it'll probably be there.
>
> XANDER
> I'm kinda feeling like this ghost is fixating on you, Buffy. The yearbook, the dreams -- you sure you can handle it?
>
> BUFFY
> Oh, I'm hoping he'll show. I truly am.

28 INT. SCHOOL - NIGHT 28 *

Xander, Cordelia, Willow and Buffy enter the school, each holding a black candle and a flashlight.

> BUFFY
> Okay, we all have our places. We light the candle and do the chant at midnight exactly. Any questions?
>
> CORDELIA
> Yeah. What if this mangled triangle thingy doesn't work?
>
> WILLOW
> Oh! I almost forgot. I made us all protective scapulas.
>
> XANDER
> Okay... So we can flip the poltergeist over when it turns a nice golden brown?
>
> WILLOW
> Scapula. You wear it around your neck for protection.

Willow digs into her pockets - pulls out four little bags on cords and hands them out. Everybody reacts. They smell.

> CORDELIA
> You expect me to wear that? It smells like grandpa breath!
>
> WILLOW
> Sorry. I didn't have much time so I had to use sulphur. Stinky - but effective.

CONTINUED

BUFFY THE VAMPIRE SLAYER "I Only Have Eyes For You" (WHITE) 2/10/98 31.

28 CONTINUED: 28

　　Everybody reluctantly puts them on. Buffy turns to them - firm.

　　　　　　　　　　　　BUFFY
　　　　　　　Okay. Let's do it.

29 INT. SCHOOL HALLWAY - NIGHT   29

　　Buffy, Xander, Cordelia and Willow enter the dark hallway. Look around the quiet school.

　　　　　　　　　　　　CORDELIA
　　　　　　　　(scared)
　　　　　　　No problem. This'll be a piece of cake.

　　BOOM! BOOM! BOOM! The hallway ECHOES with the sound of DOORS SLAMMING AND LOCKING.

30 INT. SCHOOL - CONT. (NIGHT)   30 *

　　The front doors SLAM SHUT. Every possible EXIT IS SEALED.   *

　　　　　　　　　　　　　　　　　　　BLACK OUT.

　　　　　　　　　　　　END OF ACT TWO

BUFFY THE VAMPIRE SLAYER "I Only Have Eyes For You" (WHITE) 2/10/98 32.

ACT THREE

31 EXT. GARDEN AREA OF THE NEW VAMPIRE LAIR - NIGHT   31

Drusilla is down on her hands and knees in front of a flower bed. She's digging in the dirt with her hands.

> DRUSILLA
> Maybe I'll sleep underground... Dig myself a little burrow.

ON SPIKE

Who watches her.

> SPIKE
> What about your pretty nightclothes, sweet? They'll get all dirty.

> DRUSILLA
> Then I'll sleep naked. Like the animals do.

NOW ANGEL moves to DRU, grinning.

> ANGEL
> You know? I'm suddenly liking this plan.

> SPIKE
> Fortunately, nobody cares what you like. Mate.

> ANGEL
> Oh no? Let's ask Dru-

ON DRUSILLA

Who bursts out LAUGHING. Looks up to the sky.

> DRUSILLA
> Oooooh! There's a gate... It's opening...

ON ANGEL AND SPIKE

> ANGEL
> (to Spike)
> Incoming. I love when she does this.

> SPIKE
> (ignoring/to Dru)
> What gate, pet? What do you see?

CONTINUED

31 CONTINUED: 31

Drusilla stands, her hands covered in dirt.

                    DRUSILLA
          Ummmmm.   It's black.   It wants her.

                    ANGEL
          Wants who?

                    DRUSILLA
          The slayer. It's time, Angel. She's
          ready for you now. She's dancing
          with death.

                    SPIKE
          Big deal. He won't do anything. Our
          man Angel likes to talk, but he's not
          much with the action. All hat - no
          cattle.

Angel grabs Drusilla - gives her a leering squeeze.

                    ANGEL
          I don't know about that.

                    DRUSILLA
          Oh, Angel's got cattle all right.
          Mooooooo.

She laughs. They've got some serious kundalini flying.

                    ANGEL
          Yeah. I think this whole Buffy thing
          has run it's course. I'm ready to
          focus my energy elsewhere.

                    SPIKE
          Really?

                    ANGEL
          Oh yeah. What with you being special
          needs boy, I figure I should stick
          close to home. You and Dru can
          always use another pair of hands...

Spike glares.

32 OMITTED   32

BUFFY THE VAMPIRE SLAYER "I Only Have Eyes For You" (PINK) 2/12/98 34.

33 INT. HALL NEAR LIBRARY - NIGHT   33

Willow moves down the hall toward the lounge, clutching her
scapula. The place is silent and creepy, and her fear grows
with every step...

BOOM! She's passing the LIBRARY door when it BANGS open-

     WILLOW
 Arghhhhh!

It's GILES - who is also startled.

     GILES
 Good lord, Willow! What are you
 doing here? You're not supposed to
 be inside.

Willow HIDES her candle behind her back.

     WILLOW
 Me? What about you?

     GILES
 Yes, well. I'm trying to -- I think
 I'm close to contacting Jenny.
    (re: her scapula)
 What's that smell?

     WILLOW
 It's a scapula.

     GILES
 Ahh. Did you use sulphur?

     WILLOW
 Yeah.

     GILES
 Clever. Well, hurry along. There
 may be some paranormal phenomena if
 I make contact -- you don't want to
 get in the line of fire.

     WILLOW
 Okay. Night.

He moves back into the library. Through the window - Willow
sees him return to his OFFICE where a SINGLE LIGHT BURNS.

OFF WILLOW

Watching him, troubled.

BUFFY THE VAMPIRE SLAYER "I Only Have Eyes For You" (PINK) 2/12/98   34A*.

A34   INT. GIRLS' BATHROOM - NIGHT   A34

   Cordelia enters. A beat as she takes in the dark, cold room.   *

                                                       CONTINUED

BUFFY THE VAMPIRE SLAYER "I Only Have Eyes For You" (PINK) 2/12/98 35.

A34 CONTINUED: A34

   She sets her flashlight near the mirror. Catches sight of
   herself in it. She can't help but pick at the bandage on her
   face, finally taking it off.

   She contemplates her small wound, then she pulls some make-up
   from her purse and begins to try to cover it.

34 INT. HALL NEAR MUSIC ROOM - NIGHT   34

   Buffy is moving down the hall when she HEARS MUSIC coming
   from one of the classrooms. The Flamingos version of "I Only
   Have Eyes For You". Now she sees LIGHT coming from the same
   room. Moves toward it.

   On the wall, A FLYER invites one and all to the SADIE HAWKINS
   dance - but the flyer is clearly from another time. THE
   50'S. Buffy fingers it. Then looks through the window in
   the classroom door-

35 INT. MUSIC ROOM - BUFFY'S POV - CIRCA 1955 - NIGHT   35

   The room is transformed - locked in another time - 1955. The
   RECORD PLAYS on a turntable and JAMES and MISS NEWMAN dance,
   holding on tight. Lost in each other.

36 INT. HALL NEAR MUSIC ROOM - NIGHT   36

   Off Buffy, compelled. She can't look away.

37 INT. CAFETERIA - NIGHT   37

   Xander - not a happy boy - enters the cafeteria. There are
   still A FEW SNAKES on the floor.

                    XANDER
           Oh, yeah baby. It's snakalicous in
           here.

   He takes a baby step into the room. Groans.

38 INT. STAIR LANDING - LOUNGE - NIGHT   38

   Willow sets up her candle. Looks at her watch.

   Now the same DECAYING BLUE CORPSE HAND that reached out of
   Xander's locker EMERGES FROM THE FLOOR and GRABS WILLOW.
   Starts to YANK HER INTO the floor as if it were quicksand.
   She CRIES OUT.

BUFFY THE VAMPIRE SLAYER "I Only Have Eyes For You" (BLUE) 2/12/98 36.

39 INT. HALL NEAR MUSIC ROOM - NIGHT   39

Unaware of Willow's plight, Buffy continues to watch the
loving couple dance. They spin, turn toward her. Now JAMES
looks up at her - and she sees that his FACE is now that of
a HORRIBLE DESICCATED CORPSE.

CLOSE ON BUFFY

Horrified.

39 INT. GIRLS' BATHROOM - NIGHT   40

Cordelia is still at the mirror, trying to cosmetically
conceal her wound.

Suddenly, the WOUND BEGINS TO GROW AND SPREAD ALL OVER HER
FACE. Her normally beautiful visage turns into an open,
festering sore. SHE SCREAMS and flails.

39 INT. CAFETERIA - CONT. (NIGHT)   41

Increasingly freaked, Xander moves slowly behind the hot
table - right into A DEAD EXTERMINATOR, propped up against
the wall. The exterminator's mouth and hair are TEAMING WITH
SERPENTS.

39 INT. STAIR LANDING - LOUNGE - CONT. (NIGHT)   42 *

Drawn by Willow's cries - Giles emerges from the library and
rushes to her. Finds Willow entirely SUCKED UP by the FLOOR.

                    WILLOW
              Giles!

Giles grabs her by the arm, pulls with all his might.

                    GILES
              Hold on!

After a struggle - he manages to extract her. They both
TUMBLE BACK and hit the ground hard. Willow is shaking,
terrified. Giles puts an arm around her, tries to comfort.

                    WILLOW
                  (breathless)
              Giles..?

                    GILES
              What?

                                                           CONTINUED

BUFFY THE VAMPIRE SLAYER "I Only Have Eyes For You" (WHITE) 2/10/98 37.

42 CONTINUED: 42

                    WILLOW
          Jenny could never be this mean.

                    GILES
          I know. I-
               (then)
          It's not her, is it?

Willow shakes her head "no."

                    WILLOW
          I'm sorry.

Giles takes it in - knows it's true.

43 EXT. BALCONY - NIGHT   43

Buffy, freaked, arrives in her spot where the teachers died.
She sets the candle on the ledge of the balcony - but as soon
as she touches it - she is OVERWHELMED BY VISIONS which hit
her in rapid succession:

A FLASH of JAMES AND MISS NEWMAN FIGHTING in the hallway.

The GUN GOING OFF

Miss Newman FALLING OFF THE BALCONY

James walking into the music room and putting "I ONLY HAVE
EYES FOR YOU" on a turntable.

James LIFTING THE GUN TO HIS HEAD.

44 EXT. BALCONY - CONT. (NIGHT)   44

Buffy is so startled and blinded by the visions that she
drops to the ground.

CLOSE ON BUFFY

As TWO WRETCHED HANDS GRAB HER BY THE LAPELS and YANK her
into a sitting position, revealing the terrible DEAD FACE OF
JAMES, who is leaning into her, furious. Through his blue,
cracked lips he hisses -

                    DEAD JAMES
          Get out!!

And as quickly as he appeared he is GONE. Buffy is full-on
terror struck.

BUFFY THE VAMPIRE SLAYER "I Only Have Eyes For You" (BLUE) 2/12/98 38.

45 INT. STAIR LANDING - LOUNGE - NIGHT   45 *

As the school CLOCK start to strike midnight. Willow, taken by surprise, scrambles to light her candle.

                  WILLOW
    Oh, God...

Her hands are trembling so much she can't do it. Giles takes the lighter - does it for her. Willow, shaky voiced, starts to incant-

                WILLOW (cont'd)
    "I shall confront and expel all
    evil..."

46 INT. GIRLS' BATHROOM - CONT. (NIGHT)   46

Cordy still flails - but suddenly sees in the mirror that her FACE IS BACK TO NORMAL. A beat as she hears the CLOCK CHIME. She grabs her candle - manages to light it.

                CORDELIA
    "I shall **totally** confront and expel
    all evil..."

46 INT. CAFETERIA - CONT. (NIGHT)   47

Xander is now perched on a table - well above snake level - his candle already lit.

                XANDER
    "out of marrow and bone..."

48 EXT. BALCONY - CONT. (NIGHT)   48

Buffy has also lit her candle. Despite her terror, she forces the words-

                BUFFY
    "out of house and home - never to
    come here again."

The clock stops chiming. A long, quiet beat.

49 INT. STAIR LANDING - LOUNGE - CONT. (NIGHT)   49 *

Willow and Giles look around, hoping that it worked.

BUFFY THE VAMPIRE SLAYER "I Only Have Eyes For You" (BLUE) 2/12/98   39.

50   EXT. BALCONY - CONT. (NIGHT)   50

Buffy reacts as a sudden, GALE WIND kicks up. Blows out her
candle. An eerie BUZZING sound RISES.

51   INT. CAFETERIA - CONT. (NIGHT)   51

The SAME WIND blows out Xander's candle.

52   INT. GIRLS' BATHROOM - CONT. (NIGHT)   52

...and Cordelia's.

53   INT. STAIR LANDING - LOUNGE - CONT. (NIGHT)   53

...and Willow's. Then Giles and Willow turn to see the
source of the ominous BUZZING sound-

CLOSE ON

A SWARM of BLACK WASPS which moves toward them down the hall.

ON GILES AND WILLOW

                        GILES
              Run!

They take off FOR THE DOOR.

54   INT. SCHOOL HALLWAY - CONT. (NIGHT)   54

Giles and Willow round a corner - are joined by XANDER, CORDY
and BUFFY. BUFFY BREAKS the LOCK on the door and they all
ESCAPE seconds before the SWARM pours out.

55   EXT. SCHOOL - NIGHT   55

As the gang hightails it from the campus. Xander looks back
over his shoulder - slows.

                        XANDER
              Check it. I'd say school's out for
              good.

Now they all look and see-

CLOSE ON SCHOOL

The entire CAMPUS IS BEING ENVELOPED by a CLOUD OF BLACK
WASPS. The place has become wretched, possessed ground.

56 INT. BUFFY'S HOUSE - LIVING ROOM - NIGHT   56

Giles, Willow, Xander, Cordelia are all gathered in the living room.

                    GILES
          Right then... We've definitely
          established, based on all the
          parallels and Buffy's visions, that
          it's James' spirit-

Now Buffy enters from the kitchen with a few sodas.

                    WILLOW
          So what do we do, Giles? About James?

                    GILES
          Well - he's obviously reliving the
          night of the Sadie Hawkins dance,
          when he killed Miss Newman. It's
          common for a spirit to do this - to
          keep recreating a tragedy.

                    CORDELIA
          Hey. If Sunnydale High is shut down
          forever, do we, like, automatically
          graduate?

                    XANDER
               (ignoring her)
          But why? What does he want?
               (turning to Cordy)
          Actually that's an interesting
          point...

                    GILES
               (ignoring him)
          He's trying to resolve the issues
          that keep him in limbo. What those
          are, I'm not entirely-

Buffy interrupts.

                    BUFFY
          He wants forgiveness.

                    GILES
          Yes. I imagine he does. But when
          James possesses people they act out
          exactly what happened that night, so
          instead he's experiencing a form of
          purgatory. He's doomed to kill his
          Miss Newman over and over again - and
          forgiveness is impossible.

                                                    CONTINUED

BUFFY THE VAMPIRE SLAYER "I Only Have Eyes For You" (WHITE) 2/10/98 41.

56 CONTINUED: 56

> BUFFY
> Good. He doesn't deserve it.
>
> GILES
> To forgive is an act of compassion, Buffy. It's not done because people deserve it. It's done because they **need** it.

Now Buffy goes off - her spite palpable.

> BUFFY
> No. James destroyed the person he loved the most in a moment of blind passion. And that's not something you forgive. No matter why he did what he did. No matter if he knows now that it was **wrong and stupid and selfish**. He's just going to have to live with it...

A beat. Everybody's stunned by her outburst. Finally-

> XANDER
> He can't live with it, Buff. He's dead.

Buffy's clearly upset. At a loss. She walks back into the kitchen. Xander, Willow and Giles exchange worried glances.

> CORDELIA
> Okay... over-identify much?

57 INT. KITCHEN - NIGHT 57

Buffy paces, trying to get it together. Then she finds something in her jacket - pulls it out. It's the 50'S ERA FLYER from her vision - inviting her to the SADIE HAWKINS DANCE. Now a woman's voice whispers-

> WOMAN'S VOICE (O.C.)
> ...I need you...

CLOSE ON BUFFY

Moved suddenly. Her look of agitation replaced by a look of calm.

BUFFY THE VAMPIRE SLAYER "I Only Have Eyes For You" (WHITE) 2/10/98 42.

58 INT. LIVING ROOM - NIGHT 58 *

                    WILLOW
So what next? Do we go in again?

                    GILES
Not now. The spirit is too angry.
Too powerful... We need to figure
out exactly how, **and if,** this thing
can be defeated...

                                                         FADE TO:

59 EXT. SCHOOL - NIGHT 59

As Buffy approaches the wasp-enclosed school. Moving steadily, unwavering - almost as if she were in some sort of trance.

And now the SWARM OF WASPS PARTS FOR BUFFY. She walks onto the campus, unharmed. Then the GAP in the wall of wasps CLOSES again, shutting her in and the rest of the world out.

                                                              BLACK OUT.

                            END OF ACT THREE

                                                                 CONTINUED

ACT FOUR

60 INT. KITCHEN - NIGHT   60

Willow enters - looking for Buffy.

                    WILLOW
              Buffy are you-

She stops when she see that Buffy is gone. Only the FLYER
remains behind. Willow picks it up as Giles enters.

                    WILLOW (cont'd)
              Oh, God. Giles. She went back.

61 EXT. SCHOOL - NIGHT   61

Now Giles, Willow, Xander and Cordelia arrive at the school.
The place, as before, is entirely SURROUNDED BY WASPS.

                    XANDER
              So - now what? Not even a mega-vat
              of Raid is gonna do the trick here.

                    CORDELIA
              I don't get it. Is she trying to be
              like a big loner hero or something?

                    GILES
              No. I believe she's under the
              spirit's thrall. He's calling her-

                    CORDELIA
              But why?

                    GILES
              James needs her to reenact everything
              that happened the night he killed
              Miss Newman. He wants to change
              things. Make a happy ending.

                    WILLOW
                        (urgent/to Giles)
              But it can't ever happen. It always
              ends the same. Which means Buffy's
              going in there to get shot, Giles.

                    GILES
              Yes. But remember - the school is
              deserted. There's no male inside for
              James to possess. No way for him to
              play his part.

                                                        CONTINUED

61 CONTINUED: 61

>   XANDER
> So Buffy should be safe until we can
> find a way to get her out.

>   WILLOW
> In theory. Yeah...

They all look to the school - worried.

62 INT. SCHOOL HALLWAY NEAR BALCONY - NIGHT 62

Now Buffy walks into the hall and stops where the fight always begins. She's slumped, defeated. It's almost as if she's waiting for this thing to overtake her.

Behind her, A DARK FIGURE APPEARS. A voice speaks from the shadows.

>   ANGEL (O.C.)
> Fun fact about wasps? They have no
> taste for the un-dead.

He steps forward. But Buffy doesn't even turn around.

>   ANGEL
> Not that a sting would do me lasting
> damage. It's just - tonight's
> special. I wanted to look my best
> for you.

Finally - still turned away from him - Buffy speaks. But her voice is strange - darker.

>   BUFFY
> You're the only one. The only person
> I can talk to.

>   ANGEL
> Gosh, Buff. That's... really
> pathetic.

>   BUFFY
> You can't make me disappear just
> because you say it's over.

Now she faces him. Her features contorted with desperation and rage.

>   ANGEL
> Actually...

He moves in, menacing.

CONTINUED

62 CONTINUED: 62

> ANGEL (cont'd)
> I can. In fact-

He stops. And now the SHIFT happens. His face transforms as he is filled with fear, love and sadness.

> ANGEL (cont'd)
> I just want you to be able to have some kind of normal life. We can never have that - don't you see?

> BUFFY
> I don't give a damn about a normal life.
> (then)
> I'm going crazy not seeing you. I think about you every minute.

He obviously feels the same way. Pushes it down.

> ANGEL
> I know. But...
> (then)
> It's over. It has to be.

Angel turns from her - starts to walk toward the door. This inflames Buffy's ire further.

> BUFFY
> Come back here. We're not finished!

63 INT. SCHOOL HALLWAY (FLASHBACK - 50'S ERA) - NIGHT 63

Now we see JAMES and MISS NEWMAN as they have the SAME ARGUMENT. James GRABS her arm. Stops her.

> JAMES
> You don't care anymore? Is that it?

> MISS NEWMAN
> It doesn't matter. It doesn't matter what I feel-

64 INT. SCHOOL HALLWAY NEAR BALCONY - CONT. (NIGHT) 64

Buffy burns. Shakes Angel's arm. Hard.

> BUFFY
> Then tell me you don't love me. Say it!

CONTINUED

BUFFY THE VAMPIRE SLAYER "I Only Have Eyes For You" (WHITE) 2/10/98 46.

64 CONTINUED: 64

Angel starts to cry.

> ANGEL
> Will that help? Is that what you
> have to hear?
>   (lying)
> I don't. I don't. Now let me go!

65 INT. SCHOOL HALLWAY (FLASHBACK - 50'S ERA) - CONT. (NIGHT) 65

James is devastated - disbelieving.

> JAMES
> No... A person doesn't just wake up
> one day and stop loving somebody.

Now he raises his GUN.

66 INT. SCHOOL HALLWAY NEAR BALCONY - CONT. (NIGHT) 66

Now BUFFY raises her hand and the GUN is in it. Angel's eyes widen with horror.

> BUFFY
> Love is forever.

67 INT. SCHOOL HALLWAY (FLASHBACK - 50'S ERA)- CONT. (NIGHT) 67

As JAMES' GRIP on MISS NEWMAN tightens.

> JAMES
> I'm not afraid to use it. I swear.
> If I can't be with you-

> MISS NEWMAN
> Oh my God-

SHE manages to SHOVE him back. BOLTS for the doors that lead to the balcony.

68 INT. SCHOOL HALLWAY NEAR BALCONY - CONT. (NIGHT) 68

Buffy takes off after Angel - who is almost out the door.

> BUFFY
> Don't walk away from me, **bitch**!

BUFFY THE VAMPIRE SLAYER "I Only Have Eyes For You" (WHITE) 2/10/98 47.

69 EXT. BALCONY - CONT. (NIGHT)   69

ANGEL bursts out of the hall and onto the balcony, with BUFFY ON HIS HEELS. She points the GUN at him with SHAKING HANDS.

>   BUFFY
>   Stop! I mean it. Don't make me-

Angel TURNS CAREFULLY - terrified.

>   ANGEL
>   All right. Just... You know you
>   don't want to do this. Let's both-

70 EXT. BALCONY (50'S ERA FLASHBACK)- CONT.   70

JAMES reacts with RAGE as Miss Newman continues to plead with him.

>   MISS NEWMAN
>   (carefully)
>   -just calm down. Give me the gun.
>
>   JAMES
>   Don't! Don't do that, damn it!

71 EXT. BALCONY - CONT. (NIGHT)   71

As Buffy does the same. SWINGING THE GUN WILDLY-

>   BUFFY
>   Don't talk to me like I'm some dumb-

An involuntary twitch of the finger and - BOOM! - THE GUN GOES OFF IN HER HAND. IT'S CLEARLY AN ACCIDENT. She JUMPS with surprise at the blast.

72 EXT. BALCONY (50'S ERA FLASHBACK) - CONT.   72

BOOM. The same moment with JAMES as the gun goes off. He looks at the gun in his hand in HORROR.

73 EXT. SCHOOL CAMPUS - NIGHT   73

Giles, Xander, Willow and Cordelia HEAR THE GUNSHOT. React.

74 EXT. BALCONY - CONT. (NIGHT)   74

Angel has a gunshot wound RIGHT THROUGH THE HEART. He looks at Buffy - disbelieving.

                                                        CONTINUED

BUFFY THE VAMPIRE SLAYER "I Only Have Eyes For You" (WHITE) 2/10/98 48.

74 CONTINUED: 74

   A beat - and he TOPPLES over the balcony, lands in the EXACT SAME POSITION as the teacher before him.

75 EXT. BALCONY (50'S ERA FLASHBACK) - CONT. 75

   And MISS NEWMAN topples over the balcony. Lands in SAME POSITION.

76 EXT. BALCONY - CONT. (NIGHT) 76

   ON BUFFY

   And silence - except for her terrified, raspy breathing.

   Then she turns and reenters the school.

77 INT. HALL NEAR MUSIC ROOM - CONT. (NIGHT) 77

   As Buffy walks down it, barely containing her grief.

78 INT. MUSIC ROOM - CONT. (NIGHT) 78

   HORRIFIED AND DISTRAUGHT over what she's done - Buffy moves to a STACK OF RECORDS FROM THE 50'S. She takes a record - "I Only Have Eyes For You" - from the stack.

79 EXT. BOTTOM OF STAIRS NEAR BALCONY - CONT. (NIGHT) 79

   ANGEL is still lying in a twisted heap at the bottom of the stairs. Then, suddenly, he stirs. Starts to get up.

80 INT. MUSIC ROOM - CONT. (NIGHT) 80

   With the record in hand, Buffy walks to a 50's ERA RECORD PLAYER. She places the record on the turntable. Drops the needle on.

   Buffy turns - sees her reflection in a GLASSED CABINET. It's JAMES looking back at her.

   A beat. She listens to the music - haunted. Then she starts to LIFT THE GUN TO HER HEAD.

   CLOSE ON BUFFY

   SHAKING. The gun close to her head. Her finger on the trigger...

                                                           CONTINUED

BUFFY THE VAMPIRE SLAYER "I Only Have Eyes For You" (WHITE) 2/10/98 49.

80 CONTINUED: 80

Then ANGEL'S HAND COVERS HERS.

ON ANGEL AND BUFFY

Angel, filled with compassion, gently takes the gun away from her.

> ANGEL
> Don't do this.

> BUFFY
> Grace? But I - I killed you.

> ANGEL
> It's not your fault. It was an accident.

Buffy can't hear it - protests.

> BUFFY
> It is my fault! How could I let this --

> ANGEL
> I'm the one who should be sorry, James. You thought I stopped loving you. But I never did. I loved you with my last breath.

Buffy takes this in. Starts to cry. Angel tries to comfort her.

> ANGEL (cont'd)
> Shhh.
> (then)
> No more tears.

And he kisses her. It's both a final chance for lovers to touch - and a moment of redemption.

81 INT. MUSIC ROOM (50'S ERA FLASHBACK) - CONT. (NIGHT) 81

As Miss Newman kisses James.

82 INT. MUSIC ROOM - CONT. (NIGHT) 82

Back on Buffy and Angel - and the kiss. Suddenly LIGHT moves from deep within them. Spirits RISE and vanish.

BUFFY THE VAMPIRE SLAYER "I Only Have Eyes For You" (WHITE) 2/10/98 50.

83 INT. SCHOOL - CONT. (NIGHT)   83

Giles, Xander, Willow and Cordy watch with amazement as the SWARM suddenly DISAPPEARS.

                    WILLOW
        Look... They're leaving.

84 INT. MUSIC ROOM - CONT. (NIGHT)   84

A beat. Buffy blinks, returning to herself. She's still in Angel's arms. The look of tenderness lingers on his face.

                    BUFFY
              (almost a whisper)
        Angel... ?

And his eyes go cold. He can't believe what just happened. He THROWS her from his embrace, disgusted.

And HE BOLTS, leaving Buffy totally spun.

                                      FADE TO:

85 INT. SCHOOL LIBRARY - NIGHT   85

Giles is behind the counter as Willow, Xander and Cordy enter.

                    WILLOW
        Everything seems normal. Not a
        snake, not a wasp.

                    CORDELIA
        Yep. School can open again tomorrow.

                    XANDER
        Explain to me again how that's a good
        thing?

                    CORDELIA
        I'm drawing a blank...

Giles crosses back into the office.

86 INT. GILES' OFFICE - CONT. (NIGHT)   86

Giles enters. Moves to Buffy.

                    GILES
        Are you feeling better?

A moment...

                                      CONTINUED

BUFFY THE VAMPIRE SLAYER "I Only Have Eyes For You" (WHITE) 2/10/98 51*

86 CONTINUED: 86

                    BUFFY   *
          He picked me. I guess I was the one   *
          he... could relate to. He was so   *
          sad...   *

                    GILES   *
          Well, now they can both rest.

                    BUFFY
          I still... part of me still doesn't
          understand why she would forgive him.

                    GILES
          Does it matter?

                    BUFFY
               (thinks)
          No... I guess not.

87 EXT. GARDEN AREA OF THE NEW VAMPIRE LAIR - NIGHT   87

    CLOSE ON ANGEL

    Who is WASHING IN THE COURTYARD FOUNTAIN. SCRUBBING his face
    and body RAW. Spike rolls over - fascinated.

                    SPIKE
          You might want to let up. They say
          when you've drawn blood - you're
          exfoliated.

                    ANGEL
               (sharply)
          What do you know about it? I'm the
          one who was friggin' violated. You
          didn't have this thing in you.

    Now Dru drifts over.

                    DRUSILLA
          What was it, a demon?

    Angel towels off. Throws his shirt on.

                    ANGEL
               Love.

                    DRUSILLA
          Poor Angel...

    Now Angel grabs Dru.

                                                         CONTINUED

87 CONTINUED: 87

>   ANGEL
> Let's get out of here. I need a
> really vile kill before sun-up to
> wipe this crap out of my system.
>
>   DRUSILLA
> Of course. We'll find you a nice
> toddler.

They start to leave but Dru stops - turns to Spike.

>   DRUSILLA (cont'd)
> Want to come, pet?

But Angel steers her away.

>   ANGEL
> No can do, Dru. I'm sure he'd be
> hell on wheels - but we don't have
> much time. Gotta travel light.

Now Angel grabs Spike's chair - gets in his face.

>   ANGEL (cont'd)
> Sorry. Try to have fun without me.

And they take off.

ON SPIKE

We MOVE IN as he, incongruously, SMILES.

>   SPIKE
> Oh, I will...

Then he STANDS, KICKS THE WHEELCHAIR AWAY.

>   SPIKE (cont'd)
> Sooner than you think.

And his eyes flare with INSANE FURY.

                                        BLACK OUT.

                    THE END

Episode # 5V20
Story # 4926

BUFFY THE VAMPIRE SLAYER

"Go Fish"

Written By

David Fury & Elin Hampton

Directed By

David Semel

SHOOTING SCRIPT

February 25, 1998 (WHITE)
February 26, 1998 (BLUE PAGES)

BUFFY THE VAMPIRE SLAYER

"Go Fish"

CAST LIST

```
BUFFY SUMMERS........................ Sarah Michelle Gellar
XANDER HARRIS........................ Nicholas Brendon
RUPERT GILES......................... Anthony S. Head
WILLOW ROSENBERG..................... Alyson Hannigan
CORDELIA CHASE....................... Charisma Carpenter
ANGEL................................ David Boreanaz

PRINCIPAL SNYDER.....................
GAGE PETRONZI........................* Wentworth Miller
COACH CARL MARIN..................... Charles Cyphers
*NURSE RUTH GREENLIEGH............... Conchata Ferrell
DODD McALVY..........................* Jake Patellis
CAMERON WALKER.......................* Jeremy Garrett
JONATHON.............................* Danny Strong
*SEAN (SWIMMER)......................
```

BUFFY THE VAMPIRE SLAYER

"Go Fish"

SET LIST

INTERIORS

SUNNYDALE HIGH SCHOOL
    COMPUTER CLASSROOM
    HALLWAY
    INFIRMARY
    LIBRARY
    STEAM ROOM
    OUTSIDE THE STEAM ROOM
    LOUNGE
    CAFETERIA
    POOL AREA
    LOCKER ROOM
    PUMP ROOM

CAMERON'S CAR

THE BRONZE

SEWER TUNNEL

GROTTO

EXTERIORS

SUNNYDALE HIGH SCHOOL
    PARKING LOT

BEACH
    DOWN THE BEACH

THE BRONZE

THE OCEAN

BUFFY THE VAMPIRE SLAYER

"Go Fish"

TEASER

1 EXT. BEACH - NIGHT   1

   The scene looks almost primitive, hedonistic as students
   dance around a BONFIRE to MUSIC emanating from a boombox.

   MOVING THROUGH the throng, and past the pyre, we find XANDER,   *
   WILLOW and CORDELIA warming themselves.   *

                    XANDER
         All I'm saying is, it was a stupid
         idea to have a victory party on the
         beach. It's officially nippy. So say
         my nips.

                    WILLOW   *
         I think it's festive. A party with   *
         nature.   *

                    CORDELIA
         Well, it's the team's choice. It was   *
         <u>their</u> victory.

                    XANDER
                 (scoffs)
         Team. <u>Swim</u> team. Hardly what I call
         a team. The Yankees... Abbott and
         Costello... The A. Those were teams.

                    CORDELIA
         Jealous?

                    XANDER
         No. Yes. But more no than yes. I
         mean, look at that...

XANDER'S POV - DODD McALVY

a lanky student with bad skin dances with two pretty coeds.

                    XANDER (O.S.)
         Dodd McAlvy. Last month he's the
         freak with jicama breath who waxes
         his back. He wins a few meets and
         suddenly he's inherited the "cool"
         gene.

                                                        CONTINUED

1 CONTINUED:

> CORDELIA
> Hey, all I know is, my cheerleading squad's wasted a lot of pep on losers. It's about time our school excelled at something.

> WILLOW
> You're forgetting our high mortality rate.

> XANDER
> (with pumped pride)
> We're number one!

ANGLE: BUFFY

sitting cross-legged in the sand, away from the crowd. SOFT MOONLIGHT highlights her features as she watches the tide roll in, looking positively...

> VOICE (O.S.)
> Beautiful...

She glances over. WIDEN to find CAMERON, a lean, but muscular senior as he sits next to her.

> CAMERON
> Isn't it?

> BUFFY
> Yeah. It's so... so...

> CAMERON
> Eternal. Our true mother giving birth to new life, and devouring old... Always adaptable and nurturing, yet constant and merciless.

> BUFFY
> (impressed)
> Boy. I was just gonna go with 'big' and 'wet.'

Cameron smiles at that, in a not uncharming way.

> CAMERON
> Me and some of the other guys on the team come out once a week to train in it. Swim against the current.

CONTINUED

1 CONTINUED: (2) 1

                BUFFY
    Funny. That's just how I feel most
    of the time. So, Cameron Walker...

She holds up an imaginary microphone.

              BUFFY (cont'd)
    You've just won the state semi-
    finals, what are you gonna do now?

He looks at her warmly for a moment. Buffy momentarily finds herself affected by his gaze.

              CAMERON
    I'm going to hang out with Buffy
    Summers. Get to know her.

Taken aback, Buffy lowers the "mic."

              BUFFY
    Uh, whoa. Pause button. Cam--

              CAMERON
    Hey, no pressure. I'm just saying I
    like being around you, that's all.

The look on Buffy's face tells us she feels the same way.

They hear SHOUTS and LAUGHTER, the cruel, sadistic-type, and turn to see...

ANGLE: DODD

pushing someone's head down into a metal beverage tub filled with ice water as several witnesses laugh. The someone pulls himself out, gulping for air. It's JONATHON.

              DODD
    C'mon, Jonny, you gotta hold your
    breath longer than that if you ever
    want to make the team. Somebody time
    him.

As he shoves Jonathon's head back down into the tub,

BUFFY appears.

She grabs Dodd's wrist and twists his arm behind his back in an armlock. He lets go of the underclassmen.

                              CONTINUED

1   CONTINUED: (3)   1

                              DODD (cont'd)
                    Hey!

BUFFY notices

INSERT: DODD'S FOREARM TATTOO

a grinning, cigar-chomping shark.

                              BUFFY
                    Classy tat. I take it they ran out
                    of Tweety-Bird.

ANGLE: Dodd's feet

as a delicate female foot sweeps them out from under him. He
falls, looks up to see

DODD'S POV - BUFFY

standing over him. Cameron behind him, smiling.

                              DODD
                    What's your problem?

                              CAMERON
                    Had it coming, bro.

One of Dodd's friends, GAGE, pulls him away.

                              GAGE
                    Chill, dude. A bunch of us are gonna
                    take a little night dip down the
                    beach. You in?

                              DODD
                         (eyeing Buffy)
                    Whatever.

He and Gage take off. Buffy turns to Jonathon.

                              BUFFY
                    Let's find you a towel.

                              JONATHON
                         (incensed)
                    Why don't you mind your own business.
                    I can handle this without your help.

He storms off. Buffy turns to Cameron.

                                                              CONTINUED

1 CONTINUED: (4)   1

                         BUFFY
               Isn't it fun to hang out with me?

2 EXT. DOWN THE BEACH - MOMENTS LATER (NIGHT)   2

   WE MOVE with Dodd and Gage, walking to their little sub-party
   down the beach. It's really dark and a little creepy as they
   move away from the music.

                         DODD
               Man, that chick gives me the creeps.

   Dodd suddenly stops, sensing something. He looks around.

   DODD'S POV - THE OCEAN

   We watch the surf roll in and out again.

   ANGLE: GAGE

   as he continues to trudge on. Then he pauses and sniffs the
   air with a sour expression.

                         GAGE
               Dude. What is that foulness?

   GAGE'S POV - EMPTY BEACH

                         GAGE (cont'd)
               Hey, Dodd! Dude!

   Getting no reply, he shrugs and moves off.

   As the camera PANS BACK, we HEAR a sharp SCREAM -- nearly
   drowned out by the nearby crashing waves -- and a sickening,
   wet, RIPPING sound. The screaming stops.

   Then, a SHADOWY HUMANOID FIGURE rises up from behind a dune
   to move off, toward the sea. LOW ANGLE on a PILE of TORN
   CLOTHES and REMAINS -- cartilage and skin, STEAM rising off
   it in the cool night air. Clearly visible is the tattoo of
   the cigar-smoking shark.

                                                   BLACK OUT.

                         END OF TEASER

BUFFY THE VAMPIRE SLAYER "Go Fish" (WHITE) 2/25/98   6.

ACT ONE

3   INT. WILLOW'S COMPUTER CLASS - THE NEXT MORNING   3

To the CLICKETY-CLICKING of several computer keyboards being typed upon, Willow walks among the desks of students working at their terminals. Peering over their shoulders, she's very into her nurturing teacher role.

WILLOW'S POV - COMPUTER MONITORS

All displaying PIE CHARTS in progress.

    WILLOW
 Okay, really good pie charts, guys.
 Good, good, good.

She stops at Gage's desk, whom we recognize from the teaser.

    WILLOW (cont'd)
 Gage, your pie chart... It's looking
 a lot like solitaire...
    (looking closer)
 With naked ladies on the cards.

    GAGE
 What's your point?

The BELL RINGS.

    WILLOW
 No point.

As Gage and the rest of the students file out,

PRINCIPAL SNYDER

enters, pushing through the tide of exiting students, like a salmon swimming upstream. Passing Gage, he gives him a gregarious pat on the shoulder.

    SNYDER
 Nice work in yesterday's meet, son.
 Now let's go for it!

Gage barely pays attention to him as he merges with the rest of the student traffic. The classroom now empty, a scowling Snyder approaches Willow. She moves to greet him.

    WILLOW
 Uh, hi there. Sir.

                CONTINUED

3 CONTINUED: 3

                    SNYDER
          Rosenberg. How's the class --
          everything in order?

                    WILLOW
          Well, actually --

                    SNYDER
          Great. I've been talking to the
          board -- we're having trouble finding
          a competent teacher this late in the
          term. Do you think you can continue
          subbing through finals?

                    WILLOW
          Oh, sure. I like teaching.

                    SNYDER
          Isn't that nice. You're a team
          player and I like that. A team
          player wants everyone on the team to
          succeed. Wants everyone to pass.

                    WILLOW
                (not getting the
                 segue)
          Uh, yeah, okay...

                    SNYDER
          I understand there's a problem with
          Gage Petronzi.

                    WILLOW
          Oh, good, then you know. Well,
          besides the behavior problem, he
          won't do homework, his test scores
          are, well, actually he doesn't have
          any test scores since he never shows
          up when we have--

Snyder waves her off dismissively.

                    SNYDER
          I'm not interested in any of that.
          I'm interested in why, when this
          school is on the brink of winning its
          first State Championship in fifteen
          years, you slap a crucial member of
          the team with a failing grade that
          would force his removal. Is this how
          you show your school spirit?

                                                          CONTINUED

3   CONTINUED: (2)   3

                        WILLOW
              Yes. I mean, no. I mean, I'm just
              trying to grade fairly.

                        SNYDER
              Gage is a champion. He's under more
              pressure than the other students.
              And I think we need to cut him some
              slack.

He turns on his heels and walks away. Willow watches him go.

                        WILLOW
              You're asking me to change his grade.

Snyder stops and turns to her.

                        SNYDER
              I never said any such thing. All I'm
              suggesting is you recheck your
              figures. I think you'll find a grade
              more fitting to an athlete of Gage's
              stature. Perhaps something in a 'D.'

He swivels around, and exits.

ON WILLOW

She exhales in frustration.

4   INT. HALLWAY - A SHORT TIME LATER (DAY)   4

Willow is walking with Cordelia and Xander, who is clearly
(though, figuratively) bent out of shape.

                        XANDER
              Just like that? He actually told you
              to alter his grade.

                        WILLOW
              Exactly. Except for the actually
              telling me to. But he made it
              perfectly clear what he wasn't
              telling me.

                        XANDER
              That is wrong. Big, fat, spanking
              wrong. It's a slap in the face to
              every one of us that worked hard and
              studied long hours to earn our D's.

                                                       CONTINUED

4   CONTINUED: 4

                    CORDELIA
          Xander, I know you take pride in
          being the voice of the common wuss,
          but the truth is certain people are
          entitled to special privileges.
          They're called winners. That's the
          way the world works.

                    XANDER
          And about that nutty "all men are
          created equal" thing?

                    CORDELIA
               (rolling her eyes)
          Propaganda spouted by the ugly and
          less deserving.

                    XANDER
          I think it was Lincoln.

                    CORDELIA
          Disgusting mole and a stupid hat.

                    WILLOW
          Actually it was Jefferson.

                    CORDELIA
          Kept slaves.
               (a challenge)
          Got any more?

                    XANDER
          You know what really grates my
          cheese? Buffy's not here to share my
          moral outrage about swim team perks...

5   EXT. CAMPUS PARKING LOT - MEANWHILE (DAY)   5

    A Mustang pulls into a space and parks.

                    XANDER (V.O.)
          She's too busy being one of them.

6   INT. CAMERON'S CAR - CONTINUOUS (DAY)   6

    Cameron shuts off the engine as he continues what's obviously
    been a drawn out monologue. Buffy sits beside him, bored
    senseless. The bloom is off the rose.

                                                              CONTINUED

6 CONTINUED: 6

                    CAMERON
          See, when I'm out in the vastness of
          the ocean, I never feel alone. It's
          like the sea is an old friend of
          mine. You ever heard of Gertrude
          Ederle?

                    BUFFY
              (her brain dribbling
               out)
          No. No, I haven't, Cam.

                    CAMERON
          First woman to swim the English
          Channel. Same thing. She used to
          talk to the ocean. Carry on entire
          conversations. I do that
          sometimes... Once--

                    BUFFY
              (that's it)
          Listen, Cam, thanks again. I'd
          forgotten how nice it is to just
          talk...or, in my case, listen,
          without any romantic pressure.

                    CAMERON
          Hey, I'm not about pressure. I want
          you comfortable.

                    BUFFY
          Oh, I'm comfy. I'm practically
          nodding off! That's how comfy I --

                    CAMERON
          Are you wearing a bra?

Buffy reacts, stunned, as if slapped across the face. Then:

                    BUFFY
          What?

Not hearing her, he casually brushes his hand along her arm.

                    CAMERON
          C'mon, tell me you haven't been
          thinking about this ever since last
          night.

                                                              CONTINUED

6 CONTINUED: (2)   6

                    BUFFY
          What I'm thinking about is how much
          I'd better get out of here.

As she reaches for the door handle, the electronic door lock
is tripped with a sharp "CLUNK." INSERT: Cameron's hand on
the door lock controls.

                    CAMERON
          Relax. I'm not going to hurt you.

                    BUFFY
          Oh, I'm not worried about me.

He moves in to grope her, roughly. In a flash, she seizes
his roving arm with her right hand, and slams his face into
the steering wheel with her left. His car horn blares, the
force causing it to stick.

                    CAMERON
          Ow! You... broke my nose!

As the horn continues its din, Buffy looks up to see the
disapproving visage of

PRINCIPAL SNYDER

staring back at her through the windshield.

7 INT. INFIRMARY - A LITTLE LATER (DAY)   7

CLOSE ON a chemical ice pack being squeezed until it makes an
audible "POP."

ANGLE: NURSE GREENLIEGH   *

an older, stocky woman, shakes the ice pack then hands it to

CAMERON

who holds it to his swollen nose, as he sits in a chair, an
ace bandage wrapped around his wrist.

PULL BACK to find SNYDER and BUFFY in the foreground, as she
defends herself.

                    BUFFY
          I wasn't the attacker. I was the
          attacked.

                                                      CONTINUED

7   CONTINUED: 7

> SNYDER
> That's not how it looked from where I was standing.
>
> CAMERON
> I don't know what happened. First she leads me on, then she goes schizo on me.
>
> BUFFY
> (livid)
> Lead you on?! When did I lead you on?!
>
> CAMERON
> (to Snyder)
> C'mon, look at the way she dresses.

Snyder nods. Buffy is suddenly self-conscious.

COACH MARIN, a hulking bear of a man, enters.

> SNYDER
> (greeting him)
> Coach.

Marin nods to Snyder, gives Buffy a cursory glance, then crosses to Cameron. Snyder signals for Buffy to sit.

> COACH MARIN
> How we doing, Cam?
>
> SNYDER
> Coach Marin. How bad does it look?
>
> COACH MARIN
> Well, luckily his nose isn't broken. But it sure as hell's gonna sting for a couple of days.

Snyder pulls him away for a bit more privacy.

> SNYDER
> I mean, our chances of winning the State Championship. Can we still do it?
>
> COACH MARIN
> Oh. I'm gonna need Cameron back a hundred and ten percent. He's the best swimmer I got, now that Dodd...

CONTINUED

7 CONTINUED: (2) 7

He trails off. Buffy notices his disturbed expression.

              BUFFY
    What happened to Dodd?

Snyder and Marin share a look. Then Snyder turns on Buffy.

              SNYDER
    That's none of your concern.
        (re: Cameron)
    You'd better hope that boy's nose
    heals before the meet this Friday.

The coach turns back to Cameron.

            COACH MARIN
    Walker, you better hit the steam room
    when you're done here. Try to keep
    those sinuses clear.
        (to Nurse)
    Ruthie, you take care of my boy.

NURSE GREENLIEGH

looks up from her paperwork.

            NURSE GREENLIEGH
    I always do.

MARIN

turns back to Buffy.

            COACH MARIN
    And you, try to dress more
    appropriately from now on. This
    isn't a dance club.

Marin and Snyder exit and Buffy's jaw drops.

8 INT. LIBRARY - A BIT LATER (DAY) 8

Willow and Xander are at the table with Giles. They'd been working at something as the table's littered with open books. At the moment, they patiently watch

BUFFY rant, having just entered.

CONTINUED

8   CONTINUED: 8

                    BUFFY
          So now they're treating me like I'm
          the baddie. Just because he has a
          sprained wrist and a bloody nose...
                    (realizing it doesn't
                     look good)
          and I don't have a scratch... Which,
          granted, on the surface hurts my case
          a little, but, meanwhile, Cameron
          gets away with it because he's on the
          "aren't we the most" swim team, who,
          by the way, if no one's noticed, have
          been acting like real jerks lately...

She suddenly notices the books and realizes everyone's just
looking at her. She gets it. Something's happened.

                    BUFFY (cont'd)
                    (cautiously)
          And... what's new with you guys?

                    GILES
          Thank you for taking an interest.
          Apparently, some remains were
          discovered on the beach this morning.
          Human remains.

                    WILLOW
          Dodd McAlvy's remains.

                    BUFFY
          Vampires?

                    GILES
          No. He was eviscerated. Nothing
          left but skin and cartilage.

                    XANDER
          In other words... "This was no
          boating accident!"

                    BUFFY
                    (to Giles)
          So, something just split him open and
          ate out his insides?

                    WILLOW
          Like an Oreo cookie.

The others look at her.

                                                        CONTINUED

8 CONTINUED: (2)   8

                    WILLOW (cont'd)
          Except, you know, without the
          chocolatey cookie goodness.

                    GILES
          Principal Snyder's instructed the
          faculty to keep the news quiet for
          now so as not to unduly upset the
          students.

                    XANDER
          For "students," read "swim team."

                    WILLOW
          So, we're looking for a beastie.

                    GILES
          That eats humans whole, except for
          the skin.

                    BUFFY
          Doesn't make sense.

                    XANDER
                (agreeing)
          Yeah! Skins the best part!

                    BUFFY
          Any demons with high cholesterol?
                (off Giles' look)
          Later on, you're gonna think about
          that and you're gonna laugh.

9 INT. STEAM ROOM - LATER (DAY)   9

   CAMERON

   sits alone, in a towel, gently nursing his swollen nose.

   We HEAR a HISS as fresh steam blows in, then quiet again,
   except for a faint DRIP.

   He leans back and closes his eyes.

   PUSH in on him. Closer.

10 INT. OUTSIDE STEAM ROOM - AT THAT MOMENT (DAY)   10

   SOMETHING'S POV - MOVING THROUGH THE LOCKER ROOM

                                                              CONTINUED

10 CONTINUED: 10

slowly, but deliberately, toward the steam room door.

11 INT. STEAM ROOM - MEANWHILE (DAY)   11

CLOSE ON Cameron's face. His eyes slowly open, as if he'd heard... what? He listens for a moment, then satisfied, closes his eyes again.

The door JERKS OPEN and Cameron jumps with a start.

ANGLE: COACH MARIN

framed in the doorway.

      COACH MARIN
  Okay, son. I think you've had
  enough. Time to hit the shower.

He lets the door fall closed. Cameron's heart beats like a Keith Moon solo.

12 INT. LOUNGE - NIGHT   12

Xander crosses from the hall toward the soda machine, counting out change.

      XANDER
  Too much research. Need beverage.

He collides with Cameron, who just keeps going as Xander's change spills everywhere.

      CAMERON
  Watch it.

      XANDER
    (picking up change)
  Oh, forgive me, your swimteamliness.

      CAMERON
  Loser.

Cameron continues on toward the cafeteria.

      XANDER
  Liking the nose, Cam. Good look for
  you.

Cameron stops, turns.

                  CONTINUED

12 CONTINUED: 12

                    CAMERON
            Meaning what?

                    XANDER
            Meaning Buffy must not be on your
            list of privileges after all. Man,
            I love it when you guys mess with her.

    Cameron considers attacking Xander. Then --

                    CAMERON
            You're lucky I'm hungry.

    He heads toward the cafeteria.

                    XANDER
            Cafeteria's closed.

                    CAMERON
            Not to me.

13 INT. CAFETERIA - CONTINUOUS - NIGHT   13

    The lights are off in here, moonlight streaming in through
    the windows. Cameron makes his way toward the back.

    He stops, hearing something. Moves forward more slowly.
    Sniffs, his face registering disgust.

                    CAMERON
            God, what is that?

14 INT. LOUNGE - CONTINUOUS - NIGHT   14

    Xander puts in the last of his change, pondering.

                    XANDER
            Grape, orange. Grape, orange.

    A BLOOD CURDLING SCREAM -- accompanied by the sound of
    tearing and tables being knocked over -- emits from the
    cafeteria.

    Xander starts, then heads into:

15 INT. CAFETERIA - CONTINUOUS - NIGHT   15

    Xander enters, runs well in, then stops, looking down.

                                                            CONTINUED

15 CONTINUED: 15

   At his feet lay a pile of skin and Cam's torn clothes.
   Fighting the terror welling up inside him, he opens his mouth
   to call for help.

                       XANDER
             Anybody, hel--

   He turns and finds himself face to face with

   A NIGHTMARE

   The thing has a spiny head, like a fish; palpitating gills at
   the side of its neck; large cold black bulging eyes that
   never close.

   Its gaping piranha-toothed jaw widens and lets out a PRIMAL
   CROAKING SCREECH.

   So does Xander.

                                                    BLACK OUT.

                        END OF ACT ONE

ACT TWO

16 INT. LIBRARY - NIGHT   16

CORDELIA AND XANDER

are at the table, a large sketch pad sits in her lap. He stands over her shoulder, antsy. She draws as he talks.

>   XANDER
>   (re: sketch)
>   No, its mouth was bigger, and turned
>   downward.
>   (demonstrating)
>   Like this. And with more teeth.
>
>   CORDELIA
>   (losing patience)
>   O-kay!
>
>   XANDER
>   And what's that? I said gills, not
>   dimples.

Cordelia's had it with him. She puts down her pencil.

>   CORDELIA
>   I'm doing the best I can.

ANGLE: SKETCH

-- an approximate rendering of the Gill Monster, with many differences, including, but not limited to, a too big mouth with too many teeth.

>   GILES (O.S.)
>   Is this what you saw, Xander?

XANDER

shifting restlessly.

>   XANDER
>   (unconvincingly)
>   Ye-ah. I think so... Pretty much.
>
>   GILES
>   (eyeing him)
>   You're not sure.

CONTINUED

16 CONTINUED: 16

                    XANDER
                (defensively)
            Well, it was dark. The thing went
            out the window pretty quick. And I
            was... a little shocked when I saw it
            and...

                    CORDELIA
            Go ahead, say it. You ran like a
            woman.

Xander shoots her a look.

                    XANDER
            Hey, if you saw this thing, you'd run
            like a woman, too.

Willow, holding a computer printout, enters with Buffy.

                    WILLOW
            Buffy was right. According to the
            statistics, Dodd and Cameron were the
            best swimmers on the team.

                    BUFFY
            First and second, actually. And if
            my theory's correct, that means Gage
            Petronzi, the third best swimmer, may
            be the next item on the menu.

                    CORDELIA
            God, this is so sad. We're never
            going to win the State Championship
            now.
                (an anguished insight)
            I think I've lost the will to
            cheerlead.

                    XANDER
            Raise your hand if you feel her pain.

No one does. Giles moves to Buffy.

                    GILES
            If you're proposing these killings
            are not random, that would indicate
            a revenge motive.

                                                              CONTINUED

16 CONTINUED: (2) 16

> BUFFY
> And raise the possibility that someone brought forth this sea demon from whence it came to carry out that revenge.
>   (hearing herself)
> "From whence it came?" I'm spending way too much time around you.

> XANDER
> Who hates the swim team that much?
>   (off their looks)
> Besides me, I mean.

WILLOW

thinks for a half beat, then excitedly raises her hand.

> WILLOW
> Oo...

> BUFFY
> Willow?

> WILLOW
> Jonathon! He was bullied by Dodd on the beach, remember?

> BUFFY
>   (considering)
> And he did say he can take care of those guys himself. Good call, Will. You should question him.

> WILLOW
> Really? Me?
>   (into it)
> I'll crack him like an egg.

> GILES
> Meanwhile, I think swimmer number three might benefit from your protection and watchful eye. Discreetly, of course.

> BUFFY
> I'm on it.

She exits.

CONTINUED

16 CONTINUED: (3)   16

                    XANDER
                  (to Giles)
            What about me? What can I do?

                    CORDELIA
            Well, you could go out in the parking
            lot and practice running like a man.

    Xander gives her a look.

17 INT. LOUNGE - DAY   17

    GAGE

    is at a table, with his feet up, playing with a Gameboy.

    PAN ACROSS THE ROOM TO BUFFY

    at another table, casually steals glances at him, as she
    pretends to flip through a magazine.

    HER POV - GAGE LOOKS UP

    in her general direction.

    BUFFY

    immediately averts her eyes, going so far as to reach down
    and "adjust" her shoe.

18 INT. COMPUTER CLASS - MEANWHILE (DAY)   18

    The room's dark, except for a desk lamp. Jonathon sits alone
    near the front of the room. Willow sits on the edge of her
    desk, and stares at him for several beats.

                    WILLOW
            So, you tried out for the swim team
            twice and never made it?

                    JONATHON
            I'm asthmatic. I couldn't keep up.

                    WILLOW
            You resented it, didn't you?

                    JONATHON
            Maybe.

                                                          CONTINUED

18 CONTINUED: 18

                    WILLOW
          You hated being pushed around by Dodd
          and the others.

                    JONATHON
          So?

                    WILLOW
          You wanted revenge, didn't you?
          Didn't you?!

                    JONATHON
          Yeah. Okay. I did!

Willow smiles from ear to ear, a little cocky. Now moving in for the kill.

                    WILLOW
          So you delved into the black arts and
          conjured up a hellbeast from the
          ocean's depths to wreak your
          vengeance.

JONATHON squints at her.

                    WILLOW (cont'd)
                    (weakly)
          Didn't you?

                    JONATHON
          What? No, I snuck in yesterday and
          peed in the pool.

Willow's smile slowly fades.

                    WILLOW
                    (disappointed)
          Oh.
                    (then, disgusted)
          Ew.

19 INT. LOUNGE - LATER (DAY)   19

Principal Snyder and Coach Marin walk together, talking.

                    COACH MARIN
          This is such a blow. Sooner or
          later the rest of my boys are gonna
          find out. How can I ask them to swim?

                                                              CONTINUED

19 CONTINUED: 19

                    SNYDER
          It's a terrible, terrible tragedy.
          We all feel your loss, Coach. I
          don't know two finer boys than
          Cameron and... that other one.

He stops the coach, turns to him.

                    SNYDER (cont'd)
          But I know they would want their
          friends to go on and win that State
          Championship. It's time to think of
          the team.

                    COACH MARIN
          I don't have a full team as it is.
          If we don't find someone at tryouts
          this afternoon we won't be eligible
          to compete.

As they start off again --

                    SNYDER
          You'll find someone. All he has to
          do is wear a bathing suit, right?

They clear frame, revealing Xander, who has been listening.
After a moment, he follows them out of frame.

20 INT. BRONZE - NIGHT   20

Buffy, her hair secured fetchingly into a loose bun, with two
ornate wooden chopsticks,

sips her drink as she watches

BUFFY'S POV - GAGE

shooting pool, by himself. As he lines up a shot, he looks
up and sees her.

BUFFY turns and moves past a pillar. Gage confronts her on
the other side of it.

                    GAGE
          This me and my shadow act is getting
          old. What do you want from me?

                                                         CONTINUED

20 CONTINUED: 20

                    BUFFY
                (off-guard)
            Oh, I um... Okay. It's a little
            embarrassing, but, um,...
                (blurting out)
            I'm a swim groupie.

                    GAGE
                (squinting at her)
            Uh huh.

                    BUFFY
            Yep. There's just something about
            the smell of chlorine on a guy. Hmm,
            baby--

Gage turns to walk away, but Buffy quickly BLOCKS HIM. She
appears tiny next to his large athletic frame.

                    BUFFY (cont'd)
            Okay, my sex appeal seems to be on
            the fritz today, so I'll straight
            shoot for a while. There's some...
            thing lurking around making filets
            out of the populace and I think you
            might be next.

                    GAGE
            Uh huh. And you think that because...

                    BUFFY
            It's already attacked... it's already
            killed some poeple.

Gage looks at her for a few beats.

                    GAGE
            You're one twisted sister, you know
            that? Go find someone else to harass.

He PUSHES her out of his way and moves to the exit. Buffy
glares, doesn't follow.

21 EXT. BRONZE - MOMENTS LATER (NIGHT)   21

    ANGLE: GAGE

    Walking down the deserted alley.   *

                                                                   CONTINUED

21 CONTINUED: 21

                       GAGE
                 (to himself)
            Little wacko bitch pain in the--

From out of nowhere.

                       VOICE (O.S.)
            You've got to be talking about Buffy.

Gage jumps, then sees

ANGLE: ANGEL

partially visible in the soft Glow of a street lamp. He smiles at Gage, who eyes him, warily.

                       GAGE
            How'd you know?

                       ANGEL
            She and I... had a thing once.
            Biggest mistake of my life.

                       GAGE
            My condolences, dude.

He continues on his way. Angel falls into step with him.

                       ANGEL
            She's a real head tripper.

                       GAGE
            Tell me about it. The girl thinks
            she's God's gift or something.

                       ANGEL
            Who is she, the Chosen One?

                       GAGE
            Exactly.

                       ANGEL
            You know, what she really needs is
            for someone to knock her down a few
            notches.

GAGE

enjoying that idea.

                                                          CONTINUED

21 CONTINUED: (2)   21

                         GAGE
               That'd be sweet. Anyone in mind?

                         ANGEL (O.S.)
               You're in luck, friend...

Gage turns to see

ANGEL, IN FULL VAMPIRE GLORY.

Gage's eyes go wide with terror.

                         ANGEL
               It so happens, I'm recruiting.

Fangs bared, he lunges at Gage's throat.

ANGLE: BRONZE DOOR

as Buffy exits, in time to hear:

                         GAGE (O.S.)
               Hey! Get off! Noooo!

She runs. Rounding the corner, she stops in her tracks,
surprised.

HER POV - GAGE

dazed, but very much alive. He is holding his neck, in a
daze, up against the alley wall.

Next to him is Angel, wincing and SPITTING, as if he's tasted
battery acid. He suddenly senses her and looks up. Without
a word, and before he can react, Buffy nails him with a
roundhouse kick to the face, which sends him reeling back.

She reaches up to her bun, and pulls out the two THIN WOODEN
STAKES. Her hair falls to her shoulders as she shakes it
out. Angel stops.

                         ANGEL
               Why, Miss Summers... You're beautiful.

Buffy stands, ready to attack, stakes poised.

Angel suddenly grabs Gage and hurls him into Buffy, sending
them both sprawling. He hurries off, still spitting out the
taste of Gage's blood.

Buffy helps Gage up, grimly watching Angel disappear.

                                                       CONTINUED

21 CONTINUED: (3)   21

                         GAGE
               So that... Was that the thing that
               killed Cameron?

                         BUFFY
               No. That was something else.

                         GAGE
               Something else?!

She nods.

                         BUFFY
               Unfortunately, there are a lot of
               something elses in this town.

As he takes this in...

                         BUFFY (cont'd)
               Well... g'night.

She turns and casually walks away, TOWARD CAMERA, Gage in
b.g. He suddenly snaps out of it and runs up to join her.

                         GAGE
               Walk me home?

She smiles, wryly as they continue to walk OUT OF FRAME.

22 INT. POOL AREA/SWIM PRACTICE - THE NEXT DAY   22 *

COACH MARIN

blows a whistle as swimmers dive in for a practice run.

GAGE gets out of the pool and turns to wave at

ANGLE: BUFFY

who sits in the bleachers with Willow and Cordy. She waves
back.

                         CORDELIA
               He spit it out? I thought Angel
               liked blood.

                         BUFFY
               He usually does.

                                                         CONTINUED

22 CONTINUED: 22

>   WILLOW
>   You think his eyes were too big for
>   his stomach?
>
>   BUFFY
>   I think there was something in Gage's
>   blood Angel didn't like. As, for
>   example, steroids.
>
>   WILLOW
>   That would explain all their
>   behavioral changes.
>
>   CORDELIA
>   And the winning streak.
>
>   WILLOW
>   Maybe whatever is in their blood is
>   what's attracting this creature to
>   them!
>
>   BUFFY
>   (to Cordy)
>   Any luck researching our fish monster?
>
>   CORDELIA
>   Zippo. We couldn't find any sea
>   demons that match the description
>   that Xander gave us. Not that
>   Chicken Little was much of a witness.
>   (then)
>   Oh, my.

CORDY'S POV - FEET AT LOCKER ROOM DOOR

PAN UP the body of a well-built swimmer in Speedos.

>   CORDELIA (O.S.)
>   That, girls, is my kind of...

We see the swimmer's face.

ANGLE: WILLOW

shocked.

>   WILLOW
>   Xander?!

GIRLS' POV:

CONTINUED

22 CONTINUED: (2)   22

Xander notices them and is horrified. He tries to cover himself with his hands.

>   CORDELIA
>   Xander? What the hell are you doing?!
>
>   XANDER
>   (quietly)
>   I'm under cover.
>
>   BUFFY
>   You're not under much.

Willow lowers her eyes, but keeps sneaking peeks.

>   CORDELIA
>   Get out of here before somebody sees
>   you impersonating a swim team member.
>
>   XANDER
>   I don't do impersonations. I tried
>   out for the team last night and I
>   made it.
>
>   CORDELIA
>   Really?

Cordelia smiles. He's gone up nine levels of cool.

>   XANDER
>   Figure I can keep an eye on Gage and
>   the others when Buffy can't.
>
>   WILLOW
>   Like when you're nude. I meant to
>   say 'changing.'

ANGLE: MARIN

sees Xander talking to the girls.

>   COACH MARIN
>   Harris, you can flirt on your own
>   time.

Xander leaves them.

>   CORDELIA
>   I'm dating a swimmer on the Sunnydale
>   swim team.

CONTINUED

22 CONTINUED: (3)   22

                    BUFFY
          You can die happy.
                (to Willow)
          So, Will, what about Jonathon? He
          involved?

                    WILLOW
          No, he just, uh... he sort of peed in
          the pool.

                    BUFFY
          Oh. OH.

    ANGLE: THEIR POV: XANDER

    Dives into the pool. All the girls wince.

23 INT. STEAM ROOM - DAY   23 *

    Post-practice. Xander sits in the steam room with Gage and
    another swimmer, SEAN. They all wear towels.   *

                    XANDER
          Don't you guys get claustrophobic in
          here?
                (no answer)
          I mean, what's the deal? You
          perspire a lot and can't breathe.

                                                          SHIFT TO:

24 INT. LOCKER ROOM/JUST OUTSIDE THE STEAM ROOM - CONTINUOUS 24

    ANGLE: the grate outside the steam room.

                    XANDER (O.S.)
          Or read. I mean, you could, but the
          pages would probably get all wet...

    The grate MOVES.

25 INT. HALLWAY - CONTINUOUS - DAY   25*

    Buffy is standing just outside the locker room, pretending to
    read a notice on the wall.

    The DOOR SWINGS open.

                                                          CONTINUED

25 CONTINUED: 25

   Xander comes out, towel drying his hair.

                    XANDER
          You gotta love this undercover deal.
          Twenty minutes in a hot room with a
          bunch of sweaty guys.

                    BUFFY
          Where's Gage?

                    XANDER
          He was right behind me, putting his
          sneakers on. But, they're not the
          Velcro kind, so give him a couple of
          extra minutes.

   He touches her lightly on the shoulder.

                    XANDER (cont'd)
          Tag, you're it.

   He disappears around the corner.

                                        INTERCUT WITH:

26 INT. LOCKER ROOM - CONTINUOUS - DAY   26 *

   Gage sits on a bench, putting his sneakers on. He SMELLS
   something rancid, and makes a face. He SNIFFS the air,
   checking under his arms, his sneakers...no... Trying to
   locate the source of the horrific smell, he walks to the bank
   of lockers.

   Tension escalates as he OPENS one.

                                        INTERCUT WITH:

27 INT. HALLWAY - CONTINUOUS - DAY   27 *

   ON BUFFY:

   She paces, nervously.

   Suddenly, a SCREAM comes from inside the locker room.

                    GAGE (O.S..)
          Help! Help me!

   She rushes in.

28 INT. LOCKER ROOM - CONTINUOUS - DAY   28

Buffy enters and sees

HER POV - GAGE AND THE GILL MONSTER

as the creature converges on Gage, near the grate outside the steam room.

                    BUFFY
          Get behind me. Now! Do it!

He does. She sizes up the creature, contemplating her next move, as the creature approaches. Then it stops. Buffy looks at it quizzically. And that's when Gage screams.

She turns to find him doubled over.

                    BUFFY (cont'd)
          Gage?

He bolts upright, his face twisted in agony and slick with sweat. Or slime. His hands suddenly go to his chest and Buffy watches, horrified, as his body SPLITS WIDE OPEN down the middle.

ANOTHER GILL MONSTER EMERGES from the molted casing that was once Gage Petronzi. ON BUFFY'S REACTION...

                                             BLACK OUT.

                    END OF ACT TWO

                                                         CONTINUED

ACT THREE

29 INT. LOCKER ROOM - CONTINUOUS - DAY   29 *

THE TWO GILL MONSTERS

converge on Buffy as she backs away, their webbed feet
SLAPPING aggressively on the hard floor. They BLOCK all exit
potential.

A monster moves toward Buffy. She kick boxes him in his
BELLY, and he rolls back, crashing into a locker.

The other creeps from behind. She whips around, jumps over
a bench, and grabs a LACROSSE STICK from an open locker.

While she rams it into his face, the other one slithers back
and grabs her shoulder with his PIRANHA-LIKE teeth.

CLOSE ON Buffy's face in anguish as the creature takes a
healthy bite. She CRIES OUT in pain and backhands the
creature, who staggers back, falls on it's belly and SLITHERS
down the open gate. As Buffy nurses her wounded shoulder,
the other GILL MONSTER is about to spring when

COACH MARIN

grabs Buffy and pulls her away to safety. The Gill Monster
does the same SLITHERING act down the hole.

30 INT. INFIRMARY - A SHORT TIME LATER - DAY   30 *

The nurse is finishing up dressing Buffy's wound.

                    NURSE GREENLIEGH   *
          I don't think you'll need stitches,
          but you should probably have your
          family physician take a look at it.

WIDEN to see Giles and Marin standing over the table.

                    GILES
          How are you?

                    BUFFY
          I'm definitely feeling the burn.

The nurse exits. Giles turns to Marin.

                                                              CONTINUED

30 CONTINUED: 30

                    GILES
Well, the good news is, it would appear none of your team has actually died.

                    BUFFY
But the bad news is, they're monsters.

                    COACH MARIN
How could this happen?

                    GILES
Are you saying you don't know?

Giles stares levelly at the coach. The coach sits, defeated.

                    COACH MARIN
You work so hard, you start winning suddenly... you like to think it's just you, you're just inspiring the boys to greatness. But in the back of your mind, you wonder...

                    GILES
You never asked the boys if they were taking anything?

                    COACH MARIN
                   (shakes his head)
Maybe I was afraid to.

31 INT. COMPUTER ROOM - END OF DAY 31

ON WILLOW

sitting at her computer, while Buffy and Xander stand on either side of her, their eyes glued to the screen.

                    BUFFY
                   (indicating screen)
There.

                    WILLOW
                   (reading)
"Dodd McAlvy... torn tendon. Gage Petronzi... fractured wrist... depression, headaches..."

                                                          CONTINUED

31 CONTINUED: 31

>BUFFY
>It's all here in their school medical records.

>WILLOW
>All symptomatic of steroid abuse.

>XANDER
>But is steroid abuse usually linked with 'hey I'm a fish'?

>WILLOW
>There must be something else in the mix. The point is, the boys were obviously drugged.

>BUFFY
>And Nurse Greenliegh treated each and every one of them. She must have known.

>WILLOW
>If steroids are that dangerous, why would they do that to themselves?

>BUFFY
>The need to win. Winning equals trophies equals prestige for the school. You see how they're treated. It's been like that forever.

>XANDER
>Sure, discus throwers got the best seats at all the crucifixions.

>BUFFY
>Meanwhile, I'm breaking my nails battling the forces of evil and my French teacher can't even remember my name.

>XANDER
>So what's the drill? Get Nurse Greenliegh?

>WILLOW
>   (vehemently)
>Let's throw the book at her!
>   (off looks)
>Or, a book...

CONTINUED

31 CONTINUED: (2)   31

                    BUFFY
          She's probably gone home. It can
          wait. Xander, try to find out what
          these boys are taking, or at least
          how they're taking it. Pills,
          powder, syringes --

                    XANDER
          I'm looking-around-guy.

                    WILLOW
               (to Buffy)
          What about you?

                    BUFFY
          Giles is loading up the tranquilizer
          gun. We're going fishing.

32 INT. SEWER TUNNEL - NIGHT   32

It's very dark and creepy. Buffy and Giles move through the
dank, filthy tunnel. She holds a FLASHLIGHT, and he holds
his TRANQUILIZER GUN, as they trod through the murky sewage.

Then HEAR SPLASHING ahead of them.

Buffy SHINES her flashlight in the direction of the noise,
and Giles AIMS his tranquilizer gun, ready to shoot.

ANGEL: A RAT

making its way along the wall, retreating from them.

BUFFY and GILES

share a look, exhale warily, then continue on.

Passing the OPENING to an offshooting tunnel.

NEW ANGLE - FISH-GUY POV OF GILES AND BUFFY

sloshing back the way they came.

ANGLE: GILL MONSTER

watching them from the darkness.

33 EXT. SCHOOL - MORNING   33

    To establish.

34 INT. LOCKER ROOM/STEAM ROOM - MORNING   34

    THE VISAGE OF XANDER

    Through the THICK STEAM.

    PULL BACK to see him and three other swimmers (among them,
    Sean) in towels. All of them, sans Xander, appear to be
    meditating. At least one is in a lotus position.

                    XANDER
            I'm feeling good.
                (no acknowledgment)
            Loving this swimming.
                (still ignored)
            Had some carrot juice this morning,
            a little wheat germ mixed in... Woke
            me right up. Nothing like it...
            Breakfast of state champions, you
            betcha.

    The other swimmers continue to meditate and breathe the steam
    deeply into their lungs. Xander cuts to the chase.

                    XANDER (cont'd)
            Okay, so, when do we get our next
            dose?

    Sean opens his eyes and looks at Xander.

                    SEAN
            What do you mean?

                    XANDER
            Who's carrying? I need a little
            something to improve my performance.
            Give me an edge.
                (loud whisper)
            The steroids!? Where are they?!

    The other swimmers share a look, than laugh.

                    SEAN
            You're soaking in it, Bud.

                    XANDER
            Huh?

                                                        CONTINUED

34 CONTINUED: 34

                         SEAN
                    (taking a deep breath)
               Aromatherapy...

    PUSH IN ON XANDER

    his eyes darting around, as the realization sinks in. He
    tries to bottle his growing panic.

                         SEAN (O.C.)
               It's in the steam.

                         XANDER
               Ahh. The steam.
                    (anxiously)
               And what steam would that be?

35 INT. POOL - DAY   35

    Nurse Greenliegh is in heated discussion with Coach Marin,
    following him around the pool.

                         NURSE GREENLIEGH
               It's got to stop, Carl. These poor
               children --

                         COACH MARIN
               Are you a quitter? There's no room
               for quitters on this team.

                         NURSE GREENLIEGH
               Listen to yourself! Do you
               understand what's happening?

                         COACH MARIN
               We're very close to perfecting this.
               We just need to adjust the mix.

    He exits, and she follows, into --

36 INT. PUMP ROOM - CONTINUOUS - DAY   36

                         NURSE GREENLIEGH
               You can't be thinking of continuing
               to expose the boys.

                         COACH MARIN
               They're gonna be the best. I don't
               settle for anything less.

                                                               CONTINUED

36 CONTINUED: 36

                    NURSE GREENLIEGH
              They're gonna be monsters! Don't
              make this any worse. You've lost
              three.

                    COACH MARIN
              Lost? They're not lost.

                    NURSE GREENLIEGH
              What?

He grabs her and shoves her -- she falls right into:

37 INT. GROTTO/PUMP ROOM (INTERCUT) - CONTINUOUS - DAY   37

She splashes down, surfaces again, looking up frantically.

                    NURSE GREENLIEGH
              Carl! What are you doing?

                    COACH MARIN
              Looking after my boys. They may be
              out of the game right now, but we're
              still a team.

She looks around, suddenly much more afraid. Turns, sensing movement.

                    COACH MARIN (cont'd)
              And a team's gotta eat.

Her eyes go wide -- and she is suddenly <u>sucked</u> down under thesurface.

Coach Marin looks contemptuously down at the water.

                    COACH MARIN (cont'd)
              Quitter.

                                                          BLACK OUT.

                        END OF ACT THREE

ACT FOUR

38 INT. LIBRARY - DAY   38

Xander paces the floor nervously, as Buffy, Willow, Giles and Cordelia digest the new info.

> GILES
> They've been absorbing the steroid mixture through the steam.
>
> XANDER
> Not they. <u>We</u>. <u>Me</u>. We need an antidote, don't you think? Clock is <u>ticking</u>, people.
>
> BUFFY
> Let's not break out the tartar sauce yet. It's not like you were exposed more than once.

Xander can only look at her.

> BUFFY (cont'd)
>   (hopefully)
> Twice?
>
> XANDER
> Three times a fishguy.
>
> WILLOW
> Whoa.
>
> XANDER
> What am I gonna do?
>
> CORDELIA
> You you you. What about me? It's one thing to date a lame unpopular guy. It's another thing to date the Creature From the Blue Lagoon.
>
> XANDER
>   (correcting her)
> "Black" Lagoon. The creature from the Blue Lagoon was Brooke Shields.
>   (as an afterthought)
> And thanks so much for your support.

CONTINUED

38 CONTINUED: 38

> BUFFY
> We need to find the rest of the swim team and lock them up before they get in touch with their inner halibut.
>
> GILES
> Yes, good. But we're also going to need to know exactly what was in the steroid gas so the hospital's toxicology lab can develop an antidote.
>
> WILLOW
> I'll have a little talk with Nurse Greenliegh.
>
> BUFFY
> You're really liking this whole interrogation routine, aren't you?
>
> WILLOW
> The trick is not to leave any marks.
>
> BUFFY
> Then I'm gonna visit the coach. Somehow I just don't believe that all he's been giving them is inspiration.

39 INT. PUMP ROOM - A LITTLE LATER (DAY) 39

The coach enters, followed by Buffy.

> COACH MARIN
> You've got quite an imagination, Missy.
>
> BUFFY
> Right now I'm imagining you in <u>jail</u>.
>   (as to a child)
> You're wearing a big, orange suit and -- oh look! The guards are beating you!
>
> COACH MARIN
> You don't have any proof that --
>
> BUFFY
> Just tell me what you put in the steam.

CONTINUED

39 CONTINUED: 39

He stops. The facade drops.

> COACH MARIN
> After the fall of the Soviet Union, documents came to light detailing experiments with fish DNA on their Olympic swimmers. Tarpon, mako shark... But they never cracked it.

> BUFFY
> And you did. Sort of. Why?

> COACH MARIN
> What kind of a question is that? For the <u>win</u>. To make my team the best they could be. Do you understand we have a shot at the State Championship?

> BUFFY
> Do you understand that I don't care? It's over. There's not gonna be any swim team this year.

> COACH MARIN
> Boy, when they were handing out school spirit you didn't even get on line, did you?

> BUFFY
> No, I was in the line for 'shred of sanity.'

The coach raises a gun. Buffy stops.

> BUFFY (cont'd)
> Which you obviously skipped.

> COACH MARIN
> Get in the hole.

He motions to the manhole. Buffy moves toward it.

> COACH MARIN (cont'd)
> IN. <u>NOW</u>!

She drops in.

40 INT. GROTTO - CONTINUOUS (DAY) 40

HIS POV - BUFFY

CONTINUED

40 CONTINUED: 40

nearly chest deep in murky water below the school.

HER POV - MARIN

through the hole, looking down.

>   COACH MARIN
>   You think I don't care about my boys.
>   But I do. They count on me.

>   BUFFY
>   (looking around)
>   So you're gonna feed me to them?

>   COACH MARIN
>   Oh, they've had their dinner.

ON BUFFY

She feels something brush up against her. She turns with a start, and sees, with horror

HER POV - NURSE GREENLIEGH'S MASTICATED CORPSE floats by.

>   COACH MARIN (cont'd)
>   But boys have other needs.

Off Buffy's reaction...

41 INT. POOL - A LITTLE LATER (DAY)   41

Xander and Cordelia enter to find...

>   CORDELIA
>   No one. Willow and Giles must've
>   rounded up the rest of the swim team.

Xander neurotically rubs the sides of his neck.

>   XANDER
>   Does my neck look a little scaly to
>   you?

>   CORDELIA
>   Of course it's scaly, the way you
>   keep rubbing it dry like an idiot.

He approaches the door to the locker room. He turns to her.

CONTINUED

41 CONTINUED: 41

>   XANDER
>   I need to look in the mirror. Wait
>   here. But feel free to come in if
>   you hear me scream.

She looks concerned as he goes inside.

Cordelia walks around the pool, waiting. There is an eerie
silence, and she watches the reflection of the pool water
dancing along the walls. Suddenly, she hears the CREAK of
the locker room door opening.

>   CORDELIA
>   (not looking)
>   So... Any gills yet?

She hears A SPLASH and turns to see the pool water RIPPLING.

>   CORDELIA (cont'd)
>   Xander, what are you--

As she bends down to look down into the pool.

A GILL MONSTER

is swimming along. Cordelia puts her hand up to scream,
then, realizing...

>   CORDELIA (cont'd)
>   Xander?

The Gill Monster continues to swim. Cordelia paces it as she
goes on:

>   CORDELIA (cont'd)
>   Oh, my god... Xander... Xander. It's
>   me. Cordelia. I-- I know you can't
>   answer me, but... this is my fault.
>   You joined the swim team to impress
>   me. You were so courageous and you
>   looked really hot in those Speedos.

In the background, the locker room door opens again, though
this time Cordelia doesn't hear it, and

XANDER enters.

He's taken aback to find Cordelia in mid-conversation with
the Monster. He slowly comes up behind her.

                                                        CONTINUED

41 CONTINUED: (2)   41

                    CORDELIA (cont'd)
              I want you to know I still care for
              you, no matter what you look like.
              We can still date -- or not date,
              but... I mean, I'll understand if you
              want to see other fish... And I'll
              try to make your quality of life the
              best it can be, whether you need
              little bath toys or whatever...

She has ended up kneeling by the shallow end where it swims.

                    XANDER
              Uh, Cordy?

Cordelia reacts with a start and turns around.

                    XANDER (cont'd)
              That's not me.

Cordelia looks back at the monster as it lunges from the pool
at her. She screams. Xander takes Cordy's hand and runs
with her out the door.

42 INT. LIBRARY - MOMENTS LATER (DAY)   42

Giles locks the door of the book cage in which four swim team
members are locked up.

                    GILES
              Stay calm. Either we'll find an
              effective antidote, or... just stay
              calm.

Willow re-checks her list and makes a face.

                    WILLOW
              Everyone's accounted for, except Sean.

Xander and Cordelia ENTER, overhearing.

                    CORDELIA
              Oh, I think we can safely say we
              found Sean. He was in the pool,
              skinless-dipping.

Xander looks around.

                    XANDER
              Where's Buffy?

                                                        CONTINUED

42 CONTINUED: 42

                        WILLOW
              She hasn't come back yet.

43 INT. GROTTO - MEANWHILE (DAY)   43

    ON BUFFY

    looking around for something to grab onto. A weapon, an
    escape... She listens. It's quiet, except for the steady
    dripping of the wet walls.

                        BUFFY
                   (quiet, worried)
              This is just what my rep needs. That
              I did it with the entire swim team.

    Then, behind her...

    TWO GILL MONSTERS

    rise up slowly from the water, unseen by Buffy. After a
    beat, they submerge again.

44 INT. PUMP ROOM - MOMENTS LATER (DAY)   44

    Xander approaches the room cautiously.

    HIS POV: Coach Marin standing over the manhole.

                        XANDER
              What's up, Coach?

    The coach stands, visibly nervous.

                        COACH MARIN
              Harris. How are you feeling?

                        XANDER
              A little dry. Nothing a nice lemon
              butter sauce won't cure. Where's
              Buffy?

    The coach looks over at:

    ANGLE: HIS GUN

                                                              CONTINUED

44 CONTINUED: 44

    sitting on top of something (I don't know what's in a pump
    room, okay?), off to the side between them.

                                              INTERCUT WITH:

45 INT. GROTTO - MEANWHILE (DAY)   45

    BUFFY reacts as if something's brushed her leg. Suddenly,

    A GILL MONSTER

    leaps out of the water at Buffy. She throws him off. He
    disappears under the murky water. Then ANOTHER one jumps.
    She pops him in the face, and he, too disappears. Then
    ANOTHER.   they're fast, the water begins to froth with
    activity.

                                              INTERCUT WITH:

46 INT PUMP ROOM - SECONDS LATER (DAY)   46

    The coach makes a dash for his gun, grabs it just as Xander
    grabs him. Xander twists his arm, makes him drop it.

                        XANDER
                  I don't like guns.

    He slams his elbow into the coach's face, dropping him.

                        XANDER (cont'd)
                  Elbows are neat, though.

                                              INTERCUT WITH:

47 INT. GROTTO - MEANWHILE (DAY)   47

    Buffy's breathing heavy, still holding off the Gill Monsters,
    but she's losing steam. She's not sure if she can continue.

    Then, she sees one, his head barely breaking the surface,
    making a run for her, like a shark bearing down on its prey.
    She stands as ready as she can to fend it off when suddenly

    A HAND reaches down. She looks up and sees

    BUFFY'S POV - XANDER

    stretching as far as he can.

                                                      CONTINUED

47 CONTINUED: 47

                          XANDER
                    Buffy! Hurry!

With all the Slayer strength she can muster, Buffy springs
herself up. She grabs his hand and Xander pulls her out just
as the charging Gill Monster leaps. Missing her, the
creature splashes back down into the murkiness.

48 INT. PUMP ROOM - CONTINUOUS (DAY)   48

Xander pulls Buffy all the way out. She shivers from the
combo of damp clothing and stone cold fear. Xander takes off
his outer sweatshirt and slips it over her head.

                          BUFFY
                    Thanks.

                          XANDER
                    Just doing my part for our team.

In that instant,

COACH MARIN

rises up, smashing a wrench into Xander's head. He comes at   *
Buffy as Xander crumples -- Buffy is tired, but fends him off
with a kick -- that sends him into the hole.

She dives at the hole, reaches down.

                          BUFFY
                    Coach! Give me your hand --

The sounds of eating and screaming stop her. Xander crawls
over to the hole, looks down as well.

                          BUFFY (cont'd)
                        (grim disgust)
                    Those boys really love their coach.

49 INT. LOUNGE - THE NEXT DAY   49

Buffy, Willow, Xander and Cordelia sit at a table.

                          XANDER
                    I've got to take a make-up Chem test
                    at three, and am meeting some of the
                    guys for plasma transfusions at five.
                              (more)

                                                              CONTINUED

49 CONTINUED: 49

> XANDER (cont'd)
> It's turned into quite the busy afternoon.

> BUFFY
> The fun never stops with you, does it?

> WILLOW
> Giles seems pretty confident that the treatments are going to work.

> XANDER
> Turning into a Creepy Crawler wasn't in my "Top ten list of things to do before I turn twenty."

> CORDELIA
> (to Xander)
> I just want you to know that you've really proven yourself to me. And next year, you don't have to join the new team if you don't want.

Xander looks at Cordy, touched.

> CORDELIA (cont'd)
> I'd be just as happy if you played football.

Xander's face drops. Buffy and Willow share a smile. Giles enters the lounge and beelines over to their table.

> GILES
> The people from Animal Control just left. Our creatures have apparently made a dash for it. So to speak.

> XANDER
> No note?

> WILLOW
> Does that mean we have to hunt them again?

> BUFFY
> I don't think so. I don't think we'll see them anymore.

> GILES
> Where do you think they'll go?

CONTINUED

49 49 CONTINUED: (2) 49

      BUFFY
 Home.

50 EXT. OCEAN - DAY 50

Two scaly ridged backs break water, then disappear again. PAN to see

ANGLE: A GILL MONSTER'S HEAD

it looks back at the CAMERA.

The head disappears into the black ocean.

              BLACK OUT.

     END OF SHOW

Episode # 5V21
Story # E00136

BUFFY THE VAMPIRE SLAYER

"Becoming, Part One"
(formerly "Season Finale, Part One")

Written and Directed By

Joss Whedon

SHOOTING SCRIPT

March 6, 1998 (WHITE)
March 9, 1998 (BLUE)

BUFFY THE VAMPIRE SLAYER

"Becoming, Part One"

CAST LIST

```
BUFFY SUMMERS........................... Sarah Michelle Gellar
XANDER HARRIS........................... Nicholas Brendon
RUPERT GILES............................ Anthony S. Head
WILLOW ROSENBERG........................ Alyson Hannigan
CORDELIA CHASE.......................... Charisma Carpenter
ANGEL................................... David Boreanaz

SPIKE...................................*James Marsters
DRUSILLA................................ Juliet Landau
OZ......................................
JOYCE...................................
PRINCIPAL SNYDER........................
KENDRA.................................. Bianca Lawson
WHISTLER................................
DARLA................................... Julie Benz
MERRICK.................................*Richard Riehle
DOUG PERREN.............................*Jack McGee
TEACHER.................................*Nina Girvitz
VAMPIRE.................................
GIRL....................................
GYPSY MAN...............................
GYPSY WOMAN.............................

*OMITTED
*HANK...................................
*COP....................................
```

BUFFY THE VAMPIRE SLAYER "Season Finale, Part One" (WHITE) 3/6/98

BUFFY THE VAMPIRE SLAYER

"Season Finale, Part One"

<u>SET LIST</u>

<u>INTERIORS</u>

SUNNYDALE HIGH SCHOOL
    CAFETERIA
    COMPUTER CLASS
    LIBRARY
    ENGLISH CLASS
    HALLWAY
    LOUNGE
MUSEUM ROOM
CONFESSIONAL
SPIKE AND DRU'S GARDEN/MANSION
    SIDE ROOM
BUFFY'S HOUSE
    BUFFY'S BEDROOM
    UPSTAIRS HALL
BUFFY'S HOUSE IN L.A.
    BUFFY'S BEDROOM
    BUFFY'S BATHROOM
TUNNEL

<u>EXTERIORS</u>

*GALEY STREET
    ALLEY
GRAVEYARD
GRAVEYARD - 1996
LONDON CHURCH
RUMANIAN WOODS
    ANOTHER PART OF THE WOODS
STREET
NEW YORK STREET
    A NEARBY STREET
LOS ANGELES HIGH SCHOOL
BUFFY'S HOUSE IN L.A.
    BUFFY'S BEDROOM
    BUFFY'S BATHROOM

BUFFY THE VAMPIRE SLAYER

"Becoming, Part One"

TEASER

1   ANGLE: A COBBLESTONE STREET   1

Seen from directly above at night, moonlight raking across
the cobbles. It may be difficult to tell exactly what we're
looking at for a moment. Over this still image, a voice:

>   WHISTLER (V.O.)
>   Here's the thing. There's moments in
>   your life that make you. That set
>   the course of who you're gonna be.
>   Sometimes they're little, subtle
>   moments. Sometimes... they're not.
>   I'll show you what I mean.

At that moment a man on horseback rides below us through
frame and the camera arms down to reveal:

GALWAY STREET - NIGHT

Title reads: GALWAY, 1753

The street is near deserted, a couple of BEGGARS and DRUNKS.

A pair of well heeled YOUNG GENTLEMEN are pushed out of a
doorway, someone inside growling about deadbeats. One of the
gents turns back, laughing. He is Angel.

>   ANGEL
>   We'll come back when we've found a
>   bit more cash money. Keep the girls
>   warm.
>   (to his friend)
>   Come on. We'll sneak in and take
>   some of my father's silver. He'll
>   never miss it. Eats with his hands,
>   the pig.

His friend falls down, drunkenly unconscious.

>   ANGEL (cont'd)
>   Or why don't you rest here.

Angel leaves his friend where he lies, moving on down the
street with lubricated grace. He spots

ANGLE: A LADY

                                                          CONTINUED

BUFFY THE VAMPIRE SLAYER "Season Finale, Part One" (WHITE) 3/6/98   2.

1   CONTINUED: 1

of considerable means, heading alone into a dark alley. He
starts after her.

2   EXT. ALLEY - CONTINUOUS - NIGHT   2

He comes in a few paces behind her.

              ANGEL
So I'd ask myself, what is a lady of
your station doing alone in an alley
with the reputation that this one has?

She turns slightly, a knowing smile playing across her lips.
Those of us who know her, know her as Darla.

              DARLA
Maybe she's lonely.

              ANGEL
In that case I would offer myself as
escort. To protect you from harm,
and to while away the dull hours.

              DARLA
You're very gracious.

              ANGEL
It's often been said.

              DARLA
Are you certain you're up to the
challenge?

              ANGEL
Has a challenge been made, then?

He approaches her slowly, still with a smile.

            ANGEL (cont'd)
My lady, you will find that with the
exception of an honest day's work
there is no challenge I am not
prepared to face.
                (reaches her, peers)
God, but you're a pretty thing.
Where are you from?

              DARLA
Around. Everywhere.

                                                            CONTINUED

2   CONTINUED: 2

                    ANGEL
          Never been anywhere, myself. Always
          wanted to see the world, but...

                    DARLA
          I could show you.

                    ANGEL
          Could you, then?

                    DARLA
          Things you've never seen. Never even
          heard of.

                    ANGEL
          Sounds exciting.

                    DARLA
          It is. And frightening.

                    ANGEL
          I'm not afraid. Show me. Show me
          your world.

She moves even closer to him, the sexual energy fair peaking between them as she touches his breast with her little hand.

                    DARLA
          Close your eyes.

He does.

She changes to vampface and bites down, hard.   *

His eyes fly open. He is locked -- can't even struggle. Arms about her, body jerking with pain.

She lets go and he collapses to his knees. She swoops down onto hers. Takes her finger and draws her fingernail across her chest. Draws blood.

She takes him and holds his head to her breast. Makes him drink. He does, with increasing hunger.

We see the two of them from afar, on their knees, Darla feeding Angel in perfect silence.   *

3   EXT. GRAVEYARD - NIGHT (THE PRESENT)   3

A speeding VAN wipes the frame with a roar of its motor to take us to the present day.

Angel watches something from afar. His eyes are filled with the serenity of Evil; the garrulous boy of the flashback is long gone. He is watching:

ANGLE: BUFFY

As she battles two, count 'em, two vamps. One she throws as the other comes at her. She spars with the second vamp as the first circles silently around to her back. Buffy is well in control of the situation, very focussed.

                BUFFY
    Come on. Ooh, nice try.

She easily parries another blow.

                BUFFY (cont'd)
    Now that was just sloppy. If you're
    not even gonna try, then...

She hammers him -- pulls out a stake. Just as the first vamp attacks from the rear she slams the stake home in his chest (yes, she doesn't look behind her). The second vamp stops, worried.

                BUFFY (cont'd)
    I want you to give Angel a message
    for me. Tell him I'm done waiting.
    I'm taking the fight to him. You got
    that? Do you want me to write it
    down?

Fury crosses the vampire's face -- he lunges -- and Buffy stakes his sorry ass. He dusts just like the first one.

                BUFFY (cont'd)
    All right, I'll tell him myself.

She goes over to a spot nearby and helps up a groggy Xander.

                XANDER
    I'm good, don't worry about me...

                BUFFY
    You know, you don't have to patrol
    with me.

                                      CONTINUED

3 CONTINUED: 3

                       XANDER
             Hey, I had that guy under control
             until he resorted to fisticuffs.
                   (he shakes his head)
             What is that: five vampires in three
             nights?

                                                              CONTINUED

3 CONTINUED: 3

>   BUFFY
> But no Angel.
>
>   XANDER
> You really that anxious to come up
> against him?
>
>   BUFFY
> I just want it over with.
>
>   XANDER
> I hear that.
>
>   BUFFY
> We better get back. I haven't even
> **started** studying for finals.
>
>   XANDER
> Oh, yeah, finals. Why didn't you let
> me die?
>
>   BUFFY
> Look on the bright side. It'll all
> be over soon.

They walk off together.

ANGLE: ANGEL

Watches as they go.

>   ANGEL
> Yes, my love. It will.

                                        BLACK OUT.

                    END OF TEASER

BUFFY THE VAMPIRE SLAYER "Season Finale, Part One" (WHITE) 3/6/98   6.

ACT ONE

4   INT. MUSEUM ROOM - DAY   4

We see a collection of articles for archeology and preservation. A MUSEUM WORKER takes a brush, starts brushing dirt off something we can't see. Another works beside him. Supervising them both is DOUG PERREN, museum curator.

                    DOUG
                (to a worker)
    Careful. Concentrate on this area.

Through the door well behind them enters Giles, looking about.

                    GILES
    Hello?

Doug turns, approaches him.

                    DOUG
    Rupert Giles?

                    GILES
    Yes.

                    DOUG
    Doug Perren.
    (they shake)
    Thank you for coming.

                    GILES
    Not at all. I'm flattered to be asked.

                    DOUG
    Well, I talked to Lou Tabor at the Washington Institute, he said we had the best authority on obscure relics right here in Sunnydale.

                    GILES
    He may have exaggerated slightly. Is this the...

He indicates the object we've still yet to see.

                                                        CONTINUED

4   CONTINUED: 4

                    DOUG
          That's our baby. Construction crew
          dug it up just outside of town, you
          know they're putting up those
          high-rises.

They start toward it, slowly, the camera circling them.

                    DOUG (cont'd)
          I know there were Spanish settlers
          here from way back, we've found
          plenty of artifacts. But whatever's
          written on this... well, it ain't
          Spanish.

And the camera finally comes all the way around to reveal the
artifact in question.

It looks not unlike a tomb or sarcophagus, a big block of
dusty stone carved all over with demonic runes. (It may
appear first as more of an obelisk -- it looks solid, not
like something's inside.) It stands nearly ten feet tall,
and four deep. The two workers are brushing the dust from
the cracks between the letters.

Giles comes very close, staring at it.

                    GILES
          No. Not Spanish.

                    DOUG
          Any ideas?

                    GILES
              (still scanning it)
          A few... none I'd care to share until
          I can verify... Have you dated this?

                    DOUG
          We won't have the results for a
          couple of days. I'm gonna go out on
          a limb and say "old".

                    GILES
          Yes, this predates any settlements
          we've ever read about.

He looks along the side, finds a faint line running up it.
He motions to one of the workers to hand him his brush.

                    GILES (cont'd)
          May I?

                                                        CONTINUED

BUFFY THE VAMPIRE SLAYER "Season Finale, Part One" (WHITE) 3/6/98   8.

4   CONTINUED: (2)   4

He brushes away a bit of dust. Finds a crack.

                    GILES (cont'd)
          You haven't tried to open it, I
          assume.

                    DOUG
          Open it?

Giles points to the crack he has found. Doug looks at it.

                    DOUG (cont'd)
          I'll be damned. I figured it was
          solid. What do you think's in there?

                    GILES
          I don't know.

                    DOUG
          I guess we won't find out till we
          open it.

                    GILES
          If I could ask... wait. Let me work
          on translating this text. It might
          give us some indication as to what
          we'll find inside.

                    DOUG
          You don't want to be surprised?

                    GILES
          As a rule, no.

                    DOUG
          All right. You're the expert. I'm
          pretty damn curious, though.

                    GILES
          Yes. Yes, so am I.

He stares at it.

5   INT. CAFETERIA - DAY   5

We are CLOSE ON a couple of fish sticks (wielded by Xander)
in a heated recap of last night's fight. One of them is
holding a stake (a toothpick) and one has an opened ketchup
pack held to it.

Toothpick Fishstick says:

                                                           CONTINUED

5 CONTINUED: 5

                    XANDER (O.S.)
               You can't sneak up on me!! Tell
               Angel I'm gonna kill him -- no --
               wait -- I'm gonna kill you! Die!
               Die!

     Toothpick stabs ketchup pack -- and Xander squeezes the
     ketchup pack to signify blood spurting.

                    XANDER (cont'd; O.S.)
               ARRGGHH!! Mother!!

     Ketchup pack falls dead and we widen to see Xander conclude
     his drama. At the table are Cordy, Willow, sitting on the
     lap of Oz, and Buffy.

                    CORDELIA
               Is that it?

                    XANDER
               That's it.

     ANGLE: THE FISHSTICKS

     as Xander has them take a little bow.

                    XANDER (O.S.)
               Scene.

                    BUFFY
               Yeah, that's just exactly how it
               happened.

                    OZ
               I thought it was riveting. I was a
               little unclear about some of the
               themes.

                    BUFFY
               The theme is, Angel's too much of a
               coward to take me on face to face.

                    XANDER
               The other theme was "Buy American,"
               but it got kind of buried.

                    WILLOW
                    (to Buffy)
               Are you sure you're ready to fight
               Angel?

                                                               CONTINUED

5 CONTINUED: (2) 5

> BUFFY
> Can everybody stop asking me that? Yeah I'm ready. Also willing, also able. It's the one test I might actually pass.
>
> WILLOW
> Don't say that. You're gonna pass everything. I'm gonna get you through this semester if I have to sweat blood.
>
> XANDER
> Do you think you're likely to? 'Cause I'd like to be elsewhere.
>
> WILLOW
> It was only metaphor blood.
>
> OZ
> I think you'd sweat cute blood.
>
> WILLOW
> (to Buffy)
> Sixth period, after my computer class, we'll rock on Chemistry.
>
> BUFFY
> I'm ready to rock. You're the best, Will. Thanks.
>
> CORDELIA
> Boy, Willow, you've really gotten the teaching bug. Taking over that computer class, tutoring...
>
> WILLOW
> I love it. I really do.
>
> CORDELIA
> I think it's great to do that BEFORE you go out and fail in the real world. 'Cause then it's not like falling back on something, it's like falling... well, forward.
>
> XANDER
> And almost sixty five percent of that was actual compliment.
> (to Cordy)
> Is that a personal best?

CONTINUED

5 CONTINUED: (3) 5

                    CORDELIA
          Gee, Xander, what are you gonna teach
          when you fail in life? Advanced
          loser-being?

                    XANDER
          I will teach...
               (eurotrash)
          ...the language of love.

He reaches for her, but she shrinks back.

                    CORDELIA
          Don't touch me! You have fish hands!

He moves his hands toward her face.

                    XANDER
          Come, let me caress you...

She laughs, batting away his hands.

                    CORDELIA
          Stop it!

Principal Snyder appears, looking grim as usual. He clears
his throat and everyone stops.

                    SNYDER
          That's enough of that.
               (to Willow)
          And you. Are we having a chair
          shortage?

                    WILLOW
          I haven't read anything about -- Oh!
          I get it.

She jumps off Oz's lap, sits in her own chair.

                    SNYDER
          These public displays of affection
          are not acceptable in my school.
          This isn't an orgy, people. It's a
          classroom.

                    BUFFY
               (is he nuts?)
          Yeah, where they teach lunch...

                    SNYDER
          Do you have something to say?

                                             CONTINUED

5 CONTINUED: (4) 5

> BUFFY
> This is a cafeteria. I'm pretty sure.

> SNYDER
> Always with the wisecracks. One day you're gonna go too far.

> BUFFY
> Or I could go with the classroom theory...

> SNYDER
> Just give me a reason to kick you out, Summers. Just give me a reason.

He stalks off.

> CORDELIA
> How about, 'cause you're a tiny impotent Nazi with a bug up his butt the size of an emu?

> BUFFY
> Sums it up.

> CORDELIA
> Don'tchya think?

> XANDER
> Now 'lunch' I could actually teach.

> OZ
> I can see that.
>   (as teacher)
> "Baloney. It's not a toy. Let's put it on the bread -- The **rye** bread! Careful!" Lunch teacher.

> WILLOW
>   (to Buffy)
> Do you want to come by tonight, do some cramming?

> BUFFY
> Maybe... I do have to patrol.

> WILLOW
> Again? Do you really expect Angel to turn up tonight?

> BUFFY
> No, I don't expect him to. And that's when he usually does.

BUFFY THE VAMPIRE SLAYER "Becoming, Part One" (BLUE) 3/6/98   13.

6   EXT. LONDON CHURCH - DAY (1860) - STOCK   6

    To establish.

    A title reads: LONDON, 1860

7   INT. CONFESSIONAL - MOMENTS LATER - DAY   7

    A poor but pious GIRL walks. If we see past the sanity, we
    might recognize Drusilla.

    She stops, crosses herself, and goes into the confessional.

    ANGLE: THE WINDOW

    opens between her and the priest. We see her through the
    latticework screen.

              DRUSILLA
         Bless me, father, for I have sinned.
         It has been two days since my last
         confession.

    ANGLE: THE OTHER SIDE OF THE CONFESSIONAL

    Has Angel in it, holding the body of a dead priest. He says
    nothing.

              DRUSILLA (cont'd)
         Father?

              ANGEL
         Uh, uh, two days? That's not very
         long. You must sin a great deal to
         be back so soon.

              DRUSILLA
         Oh, father... I'm so afraid.

    She is near tears. Angel finds himself both amused by his
    impromptu gig and strangely moved by the girl.

              ANGEL
         Hush, child. The Lord is very
         forgiving. Tell me your sins.

              DRUSILLA
         I had... I've been seeing again,
         father. Didn't try to, I swear! But
         yesterday the men were going to work
         in the mine and I had a terrible
         fright, my stomach all tied up and I
         saw a horrible crash, men screaming
         in the dark...
              (more)
                                                        CONTINUED

184

7 CONTINUED: 7

>			DRUSILLA (cont'd)
> my mum said to keep my peace, it didn't mean nothing but this morning they had a cave in. Two men died.

A beat as she collects herself.

>			ANGEL
> Go on.

>			DRUSILLA
>			(it pours out:)
> My mum says I'm cursed. My seeing things is an affront to the Lord. That only He's supposed to see anything before it happens. But I don't mean to, Father, I swear. I try to be pure in His sight and I do my penance, I don't want to be an evil thing.

>			ANGEL
> Hush, child. The Lord has a plan for all creatures. Even a devil child like you.

>			DRUSILLA
>			(mortified)
> A devil...

>			ANGEL
> Yes, you're a spawn of Satan, all the hail Mary's in the world aren't going to help. The Lord will use you and then smite you down, he's like that.

She is crying.

>			DRUSILLA
> What can I do?

>			ANGEL
> Fulfill his plan for you, child. Be evil. Perform evil works. Attack the less fortunate. You can start small: laugh at a cripple. You'll feel better. Just give in.

>			DRUSILLA
> No... I want to be good... I want to be pure...

CONTINUED

7 CONTINUED: (2)   7

>   ANGEL
>   We all do, at first. World doesn't
>   work that way.
>
>   DRUSILLA
>   Father, I beg you... help me.
>
>   ANGEL
>   Very well. Uh, ten Our Fathers and
>   an act of contrition. Does that
>   sound good?
>
>   DRUSILLA
>   Yes, Father, thank you.
>
>   ANGEL
>   The pleasure was mine.
>   (she starts to go)
>   Oh, and my child?
>
>   DRUSILLA
>   Yes?
>
>   ANGEL
>   God is watching you.

8 INT. GARDEN\MANSION - NIGHT (PRESENT DAY)   8

Drusilla wanders into the garden from outside, crazy and evil, the way we know her and love her. Looking at the night.

Spike is there to greet her.

>   SPIKE
>   Nice walk, pet?
>
>   DRUSILLA
>   I met an old man. I didn't like him.
>   He got stuck in my teeth.
>   (looks up)
>   And then the moon started whispering
>   to me. All sorts of dreadful things.
>
>   SPIKE
>   It's a naughty moon.
>
>   ANGEL
>   What did it say?

He enters the garden from inside.

CONTINUED

8 CONTINUED: 8

> SPIKE
> Oh, look who's awake.
>
> ANGEL
> What did the moon tell you? Did you have a vision? Is something coming?
>
> DRUSILLA
> Oh, yes... something terrible.
>
> ANGEL
> Where?
>
> DRUSILLA
> At the museum. A tomb. With a surprise inside.

He puts his hand to her head.

> ANGEL
> You can see all that in your head?
>
> SPIKE
> No, you ninny, she read it in the morning paper.

He holds the paper up. Angel looks at Dru, who smiles apologetically. Angel takes the paper, scans it. He is obviously excited by what he sees.

> ANGEL
> Oh, my...

ANGLE: THE PAPER

has a picture of the artifact on the front page.

Dru comes up behind Angel, looks over his shoulder.

> DRUSILLA
> Is that what's been whispering to me?
>
> ANGEL
> Oh yeah. Don't worry though. Soon it'll stop.

He looks at both of them, triumphant.

> ANGEL (cont'd)
> Soon it'll scream.

CONTINUED

9   INT. COMPUTER CLASS - DAY   9

                    BUFFY
          Waaahhh.

CLOSE ON: BUFFY'S PENCIL

as she taps it on her chem book.

She is staring at the book, and at her own notebook. She is tiny and helpless.

                    BUFFY (cont'd)
          This doesn't make sense!

                    WILLOW
          Well, sure it does, see...
               (looks at Buffy's
                work)
          Oh, no, that doesn't make any sense.

                    BUFFY
          It's senseless.

                    WILLOW
          It is. But at least you know that!
          So you're learning.

                    BUFFY
          Yay me.
               (as Willow looks at
                her work)
          Oh well. It doesn't matter. I mean,
          in the real world when am I ever
          gonna need to use chemistry, math,
          history or the English language?

                    WILLOW
               (re: notebook)
          Oh, I see your problem.

                    BUFFY
          I'm a moron?

                    WILLOW
          Will you stop that? You're not
          stupid. You've just had a lot on
          your mind. You can do all of this
          real easily but if you're just gonna
          give up then **don't waste my time.**

A beat.

                    BUFFY
          Wow. You really are a good teacher.

                                                       CONTINUED

9 CONTINUED: 9

                WILLOW
              (smiling)
    Good pep talk?

                BUFFY
    I got the pep.

                WILLOW
    Okay. Look at this. It's a covalent
    bond -- which means these two atoms
    are linked by this one electron. You
    know, basic linkage. Hydrogen,
    Nitrogen, Chlorine...

ANGLE: BUFFY'S PENCIL

As she places it on her book -- it rolls off and falls into:

ANGLE: THE SPACE BETWEEN THE DESK AND THE CABINET

where it lands right next to the infamous yellow disk.

                BUFFY
    Oh. Hold it.

She reaches in and grabs the pencil - her fingers almost
brushing the disk -- but just missing it.

She pulls the pencil out, straightens up.

              BUFFY (cont'd)
    Okay. I'm learn girl.

                WILLOW
    Well, you see --

                BUFFY
    Whoah. Deja vu.

                WILLOW
    Really?

                BUFFY
    The thing with the pencil-- I have
    a perfect memory of being exactly
    like --

She bends down again with the pencil -- and this time she
sees the disk.

              BUFFY (cont'd)
    -- hey.

                                               CONTINUED

9   CONTINUED: (2)   9

    She reaches in and grabs the disk. Holds it up.

                                                              CONTINUED

9 CONTINUED: (2)   9

                    BUFFY (cont'd)
              I think you dropped this.

                         WILLOW
              It's not mine. It might be something
              of Ms Calendar's.

    They look at each other. Willow pops it in the computer.
    They wait to see it come up on the screen.

                         BUFFY
              This feels kind of morbid.

                         WILLOW
              Well, I've gone through most of her
              files already.

                         BUFFY
              Does that make this less morbid or
              you really morbid?

                         WILLOW
              I had to -- to teach the class.

                         BUFFY
              Relax. I'm making with the funny.
              What does that say, "restoration"?

                         WILLOW
              It's one of her spells, I think. You
              know, she wasn't a practicing witch,
              but she did dabble in --

                         BUFFY
              Willow.

    Buffy is reading, her eyes getting steadily wider. Willow
    concentrates on the screen. Gets it.

                         WILLOW
              Oh boy.

    The camera pushes in on Buffy, as willow continues:

                    WILLOW (cont'd)
              Oh boy.

                                                              CONTINUED

9   CONTINUED: (3)   9

    Buffy says nothing.

                            WILLOW (cont'd)
                Oh boy.

                                                              BLACK OUT.

                            END OF ACT ONE

ACT TWO

10 EXT. RUMANIAN WOODS - NIGHT (1898)   10

  We hear funereal chanting, some sobbing, as the camera moves
  (looking straight down) over the body of a beatiful GYPSY
  GIRL. She has been laid out in a funeral gown. A couple of
  women in shawls kneel by her, keening with grief.

  ANGLE: A GYPSY WOMAN

  Sits in a shawl, with a painted mark on her forehead. She
  speaks in very low Rumanian, waving her hands over an Orb of
  Thesulah. As she speaks, it begins to glow.

                    GYPSY WOMAN
                  (Rumanian)
            Nici mort nici al fiintei
            Te invoc, spirit al trecerii
            Redă trupului ce separă omul de animal
            Cu ajutorul acestui magic glob de
            cristal
                  (Not dead, not not of the living.
            Spirits of the interregnum, I call.
            Restore to the corporal vessel that
            which separates us from beast. Use
            this orb as your guide.)

11 EXT. ANOTHER PART OF THE WOODS - CONTINUOUS - NIGHT   11

  Angel stumbles into frame, trying to get away from something.
  He drops to his knees, in obvious pain. Gets up and tries to
  run again.

12 EXT. RUMANIAN WOODS - CONTINUOUS - NIGHT   12

  ANGLE: THE GYPSY WOMAN

  As she finishes her incantation, the glow envelops the orb,
  which disappears.

13 EXT. ANOTHER PART OF THE WOODS - CONTINUOUS - NIGHT   13

  ANGLE: ANGEL

  Drops to the ground again, momentarily unconscious.

  CLOSE ON: HIS EYES

  As they glow briefly.

                                                          CONTINUED

13 CONTINUED: 13

He gets to his knees, groggy and bewildered, as an old GYPSY MAN approaches.

                GYPSY MAN
It hurts, yes? Good. It will hurt more.

                ANGEL
Where am I?

                GYPSY MAN
You don't remember. Everything you've done. For a hundred years. In a moment you will. The face of everyone you have killed -- our daughter's face -- they will haunt you and you will know what true suffering is.

                ANGEL
Killed? I don't...

And then it hits him.

                ANGEL (cont'd)
Oh... no.... no....

We see the two of them from a distance, the old man standing over the kneeling Angel, as Angel begins to scream.

14 INT. LIBRARY - AFTERNOON 14

Xander, Cordelia and Giles are facing Buffy and Willow. Buffy holds a few sheets of printout in her hand. Everybody is very quiet.

                GILES
What are you saying?

                BUFFY
The curse. This is it.

She holds up the sheaf of paper. Giles steps forward, takes it, examines it.

                WILLOW
It looks like Ms Calendar was trying to replicate the original curse. To restore Angel's soul again.

                GILES
She said it couldn't be done.

CONTINUED

14 CONTINUED: 14

                    BUFFY
          Well, she tried anyway. And it looks
          like it might have worked.

                    XANDER
          So he killed her. Before she could
          tell anyone about it. What a prince.

                    CORDELIA
          Well, this is good, right? I mean,
          we can curse him again.

                    GILES
          It's not that simple. This points
          the way, but the ritual itself
          requires a rather more advanced
          knowledge of the black arts than I
          can claim.

                    WILLOW
          Well, I... I've been going through
          her files and reading up and... I've
          been sort of checking out the black
          arts. Just for fun -- or,
          educational fun. I might be able to
          work this.

                    GILES
          Willow, performing this kind of
          ritual, channeling such potent
          majicks through yourself -- it will
          open a door you may not be able to
          close.

                    BUFFY
          Will, I don't want you putting
          yourself in danger.

                    WILLOW
          And I don't want danger. "No" to
          danger. But I might be the best
          person to do this.

                    XANDER
          HI! For those of you who have just
          tuned in, everyone here is a crazy
          person. This spell might restore
          Angel's humanity? Well, here's an
          interesting angle: **Who cares?**

                    BUFFY
          I care.

                                                  CONTINUED

14 CONTINUED: (2)   14

                    XANDER
          Is that right?

                    GILES
          Xander, let's not lose perspective
          here --

                    XANDER
          I'm perspective guy! Angel is a
          killer.

                    WILLOW
          Xander --

                    BUFFY
          It's not that simple.

                    XANDER
          What, come back home, all is
          forgiven? I can't believe you people!

                    CORDELIA
          Xander has a point --

                    XANDER
              (turning on Cordy)
          You know just once I wish you would
          support me and I realize right now
          that you were and I'm embarrassed so
          I'm gonna get back to the point which
          is that Angel needs to die.

                    GILES
          Curing Angel was apparently Jenny's
          last wish --

                    XANDER
          Yeah, well, Jenny's dead.

Giles moves forward like he might actually strike Xander.

                    GILES
          Don't you speak of her in that
          insolent --

                    XANDER
              (simultaneously)
          Can't you see what I'm saying --

                    BUFFY
          All right, stop it!

They do.

                                                       CONTINUED

14 CONTINUED: (3)   14

>   WILLOW
>   (to Buffy)
>   What do you want to do?
>
>   BUFFY
>   I don't know... What happened to
>   Angel wasn't his fault...
>
>   XANDER
>   What happened to Ms Calendar is. You
>   can paint this however you want. Way
>   I see it you want to forget all about
>   Ms Calendar's murder so you can have
>   your boyfriend back.

Buffy doesn't reply. She just turns and leaves the room, too distraught to deal (but not crying). Willow glares at Xander, who returns her gaze firmly.

>   CORDELIA
>   Wow. Even **I** know that was
>   insensitive.
>
>   XANDER
>   (staring Willow down)
>   Am I wrong?

Willow doesn't answer.

15 INT. MUSEUM ROOM - NIGHT   15 *

Doug Perren is at his desk, working late. He is pooled in the light of his desk lamp. The object sits at the other end of the room, mostly in shadow.

He hears something. Whispers? They drift past him, ethereal, unintelligible.

He stops working, rises. Looks around him.

>   DOUG
>   Hello?
>   (after a beat)
>   Danny? That you?

He hears the whispers again, and looks over at the artifact. Moves slowly toward it. Peering.

ANGLE: THE ARTIFACT

As he approach it, moving inexorably toward the darkness.

                                                            CONTINUED

15 CONTINUED: 15

Doug reaches it, holds his hand slowly out. Touches it. The whispers grow louder. He moves his hand away and they subside. Puts it back and they grow.

He steps closer to the artifact -- and Drusilla appears behind him in vampface. Takes a great honking bite out of his neck, hand over his mouth as he thrashes and strains.

Angel, flanked by HENCHVAMPS, strides in, eyes on the artifact.

                ANGEL
    Let's see... I'll have one of these.
        (points at it)
  To go.

The vamps throw ropes over it, securing it.

                ANGEL (cont'd)
    Be careful. I don't want this thing
    cracked. Your weak imitations of
    life depend on it.
        (to Dru, re: Doug)
    Save me some.

16 INT. BUFFY'S BEDROOM - NIGHT 16

Buffy is on the phone with Willow. As she talks, she loads her bag with weapons and crosses from her dresser.

                BUFFY
    Yeah, I'll do a couple of sweeps,
    then I'll stop by.
        (listens)
    Yeah, Xander was pretty much being
    a...
        (mildly shocked)
    Willow. Where'd you learn that word?
    My god. You kiss your mother with
    that mouth?
        (Listens)
    I don't know. I don't know what I
    want...

She sees something in the drawer, stops.

                BUFFY (cont'd)
    Okay. I'll see you in a while.

She hangs up, picks up the thing in the drawer. It is

ANGLE: ANGEL'S CLADDAGH RING.

                                            CONTINUED

16 CONTINUED: 16

Buffy looks at it, silently.

17 INT. UPSTAIRS HALL - MINUTES LATER (NIGHT)   17

Buffy is on her way downstairs when Joyce stops her.

              JOYCE
    Where are you going?

              BUFFY
    Oh. Uh, to Willows. To study. Got
    two finals tomorrow.

              JOYCE
    All right. Make sure you two study.
    Don't talk about boys all night.

              BUFFY
    Oh, we don't like boys. I mean,
    while we're studying. We like boys.
    Some boys...

As she's talking, she shifts and two crosses fall out of her
bag. Joyce bends down to get them, looks at them.

              BUFFY (cont'd)
    You know, it's funny. I've just been
    kind of... religious. Lately.

              JOYCE
    Oh. Well, you know your father and
    I are both agnostic, we always
    thought you should decide for
    yourself.

              BUFFY
    Well, I'm learning... sort of
    searching.

              JOYCE
    Well, that's good.

Joyce hands her the crosses. Not sure what to say.

              BUFFY
    Okay.

She starts to go.

              JOYCE
    Get a ride back if you come home late.

BUFFY THE VAMPIRE SLAYER "Season Finale, Part One" (WHITE) 3/6/98   28.

18 EXT. STREET - NIGHT   18

Buffy walks along.

She comes to a row of tall hedges. Stops, turning. Did she hear something?

Someone BURSTS out from between the hedges right behind her. She spins, takes an attack stance.

              BUFFY
    You know, polite people call before
    they jump out of the bushes and
    attack you.

ANGLE: KENDRA

Is the person facing her. She smiles.

              KENDRA
    Just wanted to test your reflexes.

              BUFFY
      (not angry)
    Would you like to test my face-
    punching? 'Cause I think you'll find
    it's improved.

              KENDRA
    I was on my way to your house. Saw
    you walking. Couldn't help myself.

              BUFFY
    Which begs the question and don't
    think I'm not glad to see you but why
    are you here? Wait. Let me guess.
    Your Watcher has informed you that a
    very dark power is about to rise in
    Sunnydale.

              KENDRA
    That's about it.

              BUFFY
    Great. Did he give you any idea of
    what this dark power is?

19 INT. MANSION - NIGHT   19

As the artifact hits the floor with a rounding thud, kicking up dust.

Angel regards it with excitement, Spike and Dru flanking him.

                                                  CONTINUED

19 CONTINUED: 19

                    SPIKE
          It's a big rock. I can't wait to
          tell my friends. They don't have a
          rock this big.

                    ANGEL
          Spike, boy, you never did learn your
          history.

                    SPIKE
          Let's have a lesson, then.

                    ANGEL
          Acathla, the demon, came forth to
          swallow the world. It was killed by
          a virtuous knight who pierced the
          demon's heart before it could draw
          breath to perform the act. Acathla
          turned to stone, as demons sometimes
          do, and was buried where neither man
          nor demon would be wont to look.
          Unless of course they're putting up
          low rent housing. Boys?

Two vampires take crowbars and, standing at either side of
the artifact, wedge it open. The front falls to the floor
with a great dusty thud.

Inside is the very stone demon of which Angel spoke, his face
in a horrible grimace, a stone sword sticking out of his
chest.

                    DRUSILLA
          Oooh, he fills my head... I can't   *
          hear anything else...   *

Angel approaches Acathla slowly, reverently.

                    SPIKE
          Let me guess. Someone pulls out the
          sword --

                    ANGEL
          Someone worthy...

                    SPIKE
          -- the demon wakes up and wackiness
          ensues.

                    DRUSILLA
          He will swallow the world.

                                                         CONTINUED

19 CONTINUED: (2)   19

                    ANGEL
          And every creature living on this
          planet will go to Hell. My friends,
          we're about to make history...
                  (turning back to them)
          ...end.

                                                    BLACK OUT.

               END OF ACT TWO

                                                         CONTINUED

ACT THREE

20 INT. LIBRARY - NIGHT   20

Giles emerges from his office, joining Buffy, Kendra and Willow in the library. Kendra is putting her bag on the table (note: her bag should be long and go over her shoulder like a quiver -- her sword is contained therein.)

                GILES
I've just been on the phone with the museum. The artifact in question is missing. And the curator has been murdered. Vampires.

                BUFFY
And we're sure this thing was the Tomb of Alfalfa?

                GILES
Acathla. And yes, the information Kendra's Watcher has provided seems conclusive.

                WILLOW
Okay, can somebody explain the whole 'he will suck the world into Hell' thing? That's the part I'm not loving.

                GILES
The demon universe exists in a dimension separate from our own. With one breath Acathla will create a vortex, a kind of whirlpool that will pull everything on Earth into that dimension, where any non-demon life will suffer horrible, eternal torment.

                BUFFY
So that would be the literal kind of sucking into Hell. Neat.

                KENDRA
              (to Buffy)
You think Angelus and the others are responsible for the theft of the tomb.

                BUFFY
I'd bet folding money on it.

                                        CONTINUED

KENDRA
I can't believe you dated him.
        (off her look)
I mean, he's got to be stopped.

WILLOW
We don't know where they are. They moved after Giles torched their house.

KENDRA
        (to Giles)
You did? Good for you.

GILES
It was nothing, really.

BUFFY
Willow... I think you should try to do the curse. Bring Angel back.

KENDRA
I tend to side with your friend Xander on this one. Angel should be eliminated.

BUFFY
I'll fight him. If I have to, I'll kill him. But if I lose, or I don't find him in time... Willow might be our only hope.

WILLOW
I don't want to be only hope. I crumble under pressure. Let's have another hope.

KENDRA
We have.

She pulls a sword from her bag.

KENDRA (cont'd)
Blessed by the knight who first slew the Demon. If all else fails, this might stop it.
        (less confidently)
I think.

GILES
Let's hope all else doesn't fail.
        (to Willow)
How close are you to figuring out the ritual for the curse?

CONTINUED

20 CONTINUED: (2)   20

                    WILLOW
          I need a day, maybe. And I need an
          Orb of Thesulah, whatever that is.

                    GILES
          Spirit vault for the Rituals of the
          Undead. I've got one.
                    (sheepish)
          I've been using it as a paperweight.

                    WILLOW
                    (to Buffy)
          This means I can't help you study for
          tomorrow's finals.

                    BUFFY
          I'll wing it. Of course, if we go to
          Hell by then I won't have to take
          them.
                    (sudden fear)
          Or maybe I'll be taking them
          forever...

                    GILES
          Well, Angel has a ritual of his own
          to perform before he can remove the
          sword and awake Acathla. With any
          luck, that may take some time as well.

21 INT. MANSION SIDE ROOM - NIGHT   21

    Spike is alone, pacing, thinking. We hear chanting from
    behind the door. Then:

                    DRUSILLA (O.S.)
          Spike?

    He beelines for the chair, gets in just before she enters the
    room.

                    DRUSILLA
          Spike, sweetie, the fun's about to
          begin.

                    SPIKE
          Is it? Seems more to me like the
          fun's about to end.

                    DRUSILLA
          Don't be all gloomy.

                                                         CONTINUED

BUFFY THE VAMPIRE SLAYER "Season Finale, Part One" (WHITE) 3/6/98   34.

21   CONTINUED: 21

                    SPIKE
          Darling, if this works, everything
          changes. Think about it. In this
          world, we can be kings. In the
          next...

                    DRUSILLA
          My Spikey's getting cold feet. Don't
          you worry about the next world.
          You'll always have me...

                    SPIKE
          Will I?

     She doesn't answer. A SCREAM emerges from the main room --
     that of a young man.

                    DRUSILLA
          Oh! The blood ritual! To cleanse
          Angel. Let's go and see.

                    SPIKE
               (giving in)
          Well, if there's blood...

     They go out into:

22   INT. MANSION - NIGHT   22

     In the main chamber, where the statue stands free of its
     casing at one end.

     At the other, Angel waits as two vampires bring the young man
     before him. Angel looks at him, eyes glowing in reverent
     reverie.

                    ANGEL
          I will drink... the blood will wash
          in me, over me and I will be
          cleansed, I will be worthy to free
          Acathla.
               (to Spike and Dru)
          Bear witness, as I ascend.
               (looking at the man)
          As I become.

     He changes to vampface. Bites.

23   EXT. NEW YORK STREET - NIGHT (1996)   23

     A title reads: MANHATTAN, 1996

                                                              CONTINUED

23 CONTINUED: 23

It's a dark, grimy district -- not many people out, and none with too much money.

We pick up a HOMELESS MAN moving along in the shadows. He stops at a group of garbage cans, sees:

ANGLE: A RAT

Scurrying among them.

The man makes a dive for the rat, but it gets away and he lands in a clatter among the cans. We see that it is Angel. He looks utterly lost and destitute -- not entirely sane, even.

He sits, defeated as another figure approaches him. WHISTLER is young in appearance, and wearing a bad suit over a loud shirt. He looks like a bottom-ranked mafioso. His manner, like his outfit, is loud and grating.

                    WHISTLER
          God, are you disgusting.

Angel starts, not used to being talked to. He starts to crawl back into the shadows.

                    WHISTLER (cont'd)
          This is really an unforgettable
          smell. This is the stench of death
          you're giving off here. And the look
          says crazy homeless guy, it's not
          good.

                    ANGEL
          Get away from me.

                    WHISTLER
          What are you gonna do, biteme? Oh,
          horrors! A Vampire!

Angel stops, staring at him.

                    WHISTLER (cont'd)
          Oh, but you're not gonna bite me
          'cause of your poor tortured **soul**,
          it's so sad, a vampire with a soul,
          how poignant, I may physically vomit
          right here.

                    ANGEL
          Who are you?

CONTINUED

BUFFY THE VAMPIRE SLAYER "Season Finale, Part One" (WHITE) 3/6/98   36.

23   CONTINUED: (2)   23

                    WHISTLER
              Let's take a walk. Come on.

He starts to help Angel up. Angel is clearly weak. As he
gets to his feet a respectable PASSERBY stares at the pair.

                    WHISTLER (cont'd)
                    (to the
                     passerby)
              What? Yes, he's my lover, you
              mustn't **judge us!**

The passerby scurries off.

                    WHISTLER (cont'd)
              God, I hate people.

24   EXT. A NEARBY STREET - MINUTES LATER - NIGHT   24

The two are walking together. Whistler's doing most of the
talking.

                    WHISTLER
              What are you eating, like a rat once
              a month? You're skin and bones here.
              Butcher shops are throwing away more
              blood in a day than you could stand.
              Good blood. You lived in the world
              a little bit you'd know that.

                    ANGEL
              I want to know who you are.

Whistler stops, faces him.

                    WHISTLER
              And I want to know who you are.

                    ANGEL
              You already do.

                    WHISTLER
              Not yet. I'm looking to find out.
              'Cause you could go either way here.

                    ANGEL
              I don't understand you.

                    WHISTLER
              Nobody understands me. It's my
              curse.

                                                              CONTINUED

24 CONTINUED: 24

He walks a few feet away, to a SABRETT VENDER.

>   WHISTLER (cont'd)
>   (to the
>   vender)
> Dog me.
>   (to Angel)
> There are three kinds of people that
> no one understands. Geniuses,
> madmen, and guys that mumble. My
> name is Whistler. Anyway, lately it
> is. My real name is hard to
> pronounce unless you're a dolphin.

He pays, takes a big bite out of his dog.

>   ANGEL
> You're not a vampire.

>   WHISTLER
> A demon, technically. But I'm not a
> bad guy -- not all demons are
> dedicated to the destruction of all
> life. Someone has to maintain
> balance, you know. Good and evil
> can't exist without each other, blah
> blah blah. I'm not like a good fairy
> or anything, I'm just trying to make
> it all balance -- do I come off
> defensive?

>   ANGEL
> What did you mean, I could go either
> way?

>   WHISTLER
> I mean you could become an even more
> useless rodent than you are right
> now, or you could become... someone.
> A person. Someone to be counted.

>   ANGEL
> I just want to be left alone.

>   WHISTLER
> You've been alone for what, ninety
> years? And what an impressive
> package you are. The stink guy.

>   ANGEL
> You don't know what I have to deal
> with. What I've done.

CONTINUED

24 CONTINUED: (2)   24

                    WHISTLER
          You're annoying me! The self pity
          thing is not gonna bring in the
          chicks. It's a bore.

                    ANGEL
          What do you want from me?

                    WHISTLER
          I want you to see something. It's
          happening very soon, we'd need to
          leave now. You see, and then you
          tell me what you want to do.

                    ANGEL
          Where is it?

25 EXT. LOS ANGELES HIGH SCHOOL - DAY (1996)   25

Title: LOS ANGELES, 1996

We see Angel in the shadows (or indoors, depending on
location) looking out into the bright sunlit courtyard. We
see, as he does:

ANGLE: BUFFY

Walking along with her FRIENDS, talking. She is all of
fifteen, completely carefree and not a little superficial.

                    BUFFY
          So, I'm like, "Dad, you want me to go
          to the dance in an outfit I've
          already worn? Why do you hate me?"

                    GIRL
          Is Tyler taking you?

                    BUFFY
          Oh my god! Where were you when I got
          over Tyler? He's of the past.
          Tyler would have to crawl on his
          hands and knees to get me to go to
          the dance with him. Which he's
          actually supposed to do after
          practice, so I'm gonna wait.

                    GIRL
          Okay. See you later.

They go, Buffy saying to each one:

                                                                     CONTINUED

25 CONTINUED: 25

                    BUFFY
          Call me. Call me. Call me.

     They all go and Buffy sits. She has waited for a moment when
     a MAN approaches her in a dark, rumpled suit. He looks
     vaguely nervous, and deadly serious. His name is MERRICK.

                    MERRICK
          Buffy Summers?

                    BUFFY
          Yeah? Hi. What?

                    MERRICK
          I need to speak with you.

                    BUFFY
          You're not from Macy's, are you?
          'Cause I meant to pay for that
          lipstick...

                    MERRICK
          There isn't much time. You must come
          with me. Your destiny awaits.

                    BUFFY
          I don't have a destiny. I'm destiny-
          free. Really.

                    MERRICK
          Yes, you have. You are the chosen
          one. You alone can stop them.

                    BUFFY
          Who?

                    MERRICK
          The vampires.

     Buffy stares at him for a good long while, a polite smile
     playing on her lips, trying to come up with a response.
     Finally she breaks down into:

                    BUFFY
          Huh?

26   EXT. GRAVEYARD - NIGHT (1996)   26

     Buffy crashes into frame, wide eyed and terrified, a VAMPIRE
     right on top of her.

                                                           CONTINUED

26 CONTINUED: 26

                         BUFFY
               AAAAAAGHHHH!

It snarls and snaps, trying to bite her. She throws it off.

She goes scrambling for a stake on her hands and knees --

                         BUFFY (cont'd)
               Oh god oh god oh god --

She comes up with it as the vampire charges her again -- she
instinctively flips it onto its back.

                         BUFFY (cont'd)
               Whoah! Wow.

Collecting herself, she drops down and plunges the stake into
its chest, pulling it out again.

The vampire screams, but nothing happens.

                         BUFFY (cont'd)
               Ooh, that's not the heart...

She tries again, and the vampire's dying rasp tells her she's
hit home.

ANGLE: THE VAMPIRE

Explodes into dust.

                         BUFFY (cont'd)
               GAAAGHHH!

she starts back from this unexpected effect, stays panting on
the grass. We see a pair of legs come into frame near her.

                         MERRICK
               You see? You see your power?

She says nothing, still staring at the spot where the vampire
was.

ANGLE: ANGEL

Watching from the shadows.

27 EXT./INT. BUFFY'S BEDROOM IN L.A. (1996) - NIGHT   27

   We see in from the outside. Buffy enters her bedroom,
   followed by Joyce.

                                                          CONTINUED

27 CONTINUED: 27

                    JOYCE
          Why didn't you call?

                    BUFFY
          I'm sorry, Mom, I didn't know it was
          so late. Tyler and I were talking.

                    JOYCE
          That boy is irresponsible.

                    BUFFY
          It's my fault.

                    JOYCE
          You know we worry, that's all.
          Dinner's in ten minutes.

                    BUFFY
          Okay.

Buffy moves into the bathroom, shutting the door behind her.

ANGLE: ANGEL

Watches, obviously feeling for her.

28 EXT./INT. BUFFY'S BATHROOM IN L.A. (1996) - NIGHT   28

ANGLE: BUFFY THROUGH THE WINDOW

We see her go to the sink, take off her jacket. Splash her face. She is very shaken. Over her silent actions we hear the voices of her parents.

                    HANK (O.S.)
          Did she say where she was?

                    JOYCE (O.S.)
          She was with Tyler.

                    HANK (O.S.)
          I don't want her seeing him anymore.
          Period.

                    JOYCE (O.S.)
          You're over reacting, dear.

                    HANK (O.S.)
          Don't do that! Don't talk to me like
          I'm a kid.

CONTINUED

28 CONTINUED: 28

                    JOYCE (O.S.)
          I don't -- forget it.

                    HANK (O.S.)
          Just because you can't discipline
          her, I have to be the ogre.

                    JOYCE (O.S.)
          I'm not having this conversation
          again. All right?

     Buffy stays in the bathroom, silent.

29   INT. TUNNEL - NIGHT   29

     Angel jumps down at one end. At the other, Whistler waits.
     Angel slowly approaches him.

                    WHISTLER
          She's gonna have it tough, that
          Slayer. She's just a kid. And the
          world is full of big bad things.

                    ANGEL
          I want to help her. I want to... I
          want to become someone. I want to
          help.

                    WHISTLER
          Jeez, look at you. She must be
          prettier than the last Slayer.
                    (Angel looks down)
          It's not gonna be easy. The more you
          live in the world the more you see
          how apart from it you are. And this
          is dangerous work. Right now you
          couldn't go three rounds with a fruit
          fly.

                    ANGEL
          I want to learn from you.

                    WHISTLER
          Okay.

     They start off together.

                    ANGEL
          But I don't want to dress like you.

                    WHISTLER
          See? Again you're annoying me.

30 INT. MANSION - NIGHT (PRESENT DAY)   30

Angel lifts his face, blood on his mouth, from his victim. He walks slowly to the statue, the others watching him.

He looks at his hand. It too has blood on it.

            ANGEL
    Everything that I am, everything that
    I have done, has led me here. This
    night. This act.
        (to the statue)
    You will be free.

In a lightning-quick motion, he grabs the hilt of the sword.

White light fills the room.

                                  BLACK OUT.

                END OF ACT THREE

BUFFY THE VAMPIRE SLAYER "Season Finale, Part One" (WHITE) 3/6/98 44.

ACT FOUR

31 INT. MANSION - NIGHT   31

   The light still fills the room, along with a crackling
   energy -- that stops in an instant as Angel is thrown back to
   the floor. He seems to have gotten an enormous electrical
   shock, and his vampface is gone.

   The sword is still in the statue. Angel looks at it,
   uncomprehending.

                    SPIKE
                 (singsong)
             Someone wasn't worthy...

   Angel rises, furious.

                    ANGEL
             The ritual. There must be something
             I missed. The incantations, the
             blood... Dammit! I don't know...

                    DRUSILLA
             This is so disappointing. What are
             we going to do?

   He stops. Turns to them.

                    ANGEL
             What we always do in a time of
             trouble. Turn to an old friend.
             We'll have our Armageddon, I swear.

   He grabs an old vase from off a pedestal, rage and impatience
   seething in him, and hurls it against the wall.

   It shatters.

32 INT. ENGLISH CLASS - MORNING   32

   The morning sunlight brightly rakes the classroom. Buffy is
   seated, along with Xander and Willow and Cordy, amidst the
   other students. They are all taking their final exam,
   scribbling in their bluebooks. The room is silent.

   The teacher sits at his desk, reading.

BUFFY THE VAMPIRE SLAYER "Season Finale, Part One" (WHITE) 3/6/98   45.

33   INT. HALLWAY - CONTINUOUS - DAY   33

The Camera dolly's behind a figure in the hall. She moves
slowly, a shawl wrapped around her head, her clothes dark and
shabby.

34   INT. CLASSROOM - CONTINUOUS - DAY   34

Buffy is frowning at her test when she hears:

                  VAMPIRE (O.S.)
    Tonight. Sundown. In the graveyard.

                  TEACHER
        (rising)
    Excuse me...

Buffy looks up. The woman is standing in the classroom --
speaks to Buffy --

                  VAMPIRE
    You will come to him.

She pulls off her shawl, revealing her vamp visage, and moves
toward Buffy, deliberately stepping into the sunlight. She
begins to smoke. Kids start trying to move away. Buffy
can't take her eyes off the vampire.

                  VAMPIRE (cont'd)
    You will come to him or more will
    die! Tonight!

Flames engulf her as kids scream and get out of there.

                  VAMPIRE (cont'd)
    His hour is at hand!

And she's gone, flamed out. The classroom is nearly empty
except for our principals. Buffy still hasn't moved.

35   INT. LIBRARY - JUST BEFORE SUNSET   35

The gang's all here (minus Oz, plus Kendra). Willow is deep
in a pile of books.

                  BUFFY
    She said more would die. I have to
    go.

                  KENDRA
    And I should go with you.

                                                CONTINUED

35 CONTINUED: 35

> BUFFY
> I need you here. Just in case. I'll be all right. As long as Angel's fighting me he's not doing his end of the world ritual and that's good. And with any luck... Willow? What do you think?

> WILLOW
> I'm not sure. I just want to cross check --

> BUFFY
> We don't have time. If this is gonna work I need it to work now.

> WILLOW
> I need maybe half an hour once we're set up.

> GILES
> Which means you just have to hold Angel off. Don't let him close on you. If the curse succeeds, you'll know.

> CORDELIA
> Why don't you just wait **here** to find out if it worked? See if he phones you?

> BUFFY
> I can't risk him killing more people.

> XANDER
> What if he shows up with an army?

> BUFFY
> I'll run away.

> KENDRA
> A Slayer never runs aw --
>   (off their looks)
> Good plan.

> BUFFY
> I'd better go.

> XANDER
> Please be careful.

> BUFFY
> I will.

CONTINUED

BUFFY THE VAMPIRE SLAYER "Season Finale, Part One" (WHITE) 3/6/98   47.

35 CONTINUED: (2)   35

Buffy starts for the door. Kendra runs up to her, hands her
a stake.

                    KENDRA
          Here. In case the curse does not
          succeed... This is my lucky stake.
          I have killed many vampires with it.
                    (in a low voice)
          I call it Mister Pointy.

                    BUFFY
          You named your stake.

                    KENDRA
                    (embarrassed)
          Yes.

                    BUFFY
          Remind me to get you a stuffed animal.
                    (puts the stake in
                     her jacket)
          Thanks.

                    KENDRA
          Watch your back.

Buffy exits.

36 EXT. GRAVEYARD - NIGHT   36

Buffy makes her way along in the dark. After a time:

                    ANGEL
          Hello, lover.

She turns to face him. He stands some twenty feet away,
grinning nonchalantly.

They begin circling each other, slowly.

                    ANGEL (cont'd)
          I wasn't sure you'd come.

                    BUFFY
          After your immolation-o-gram? Come
          on, I had to show. But shouldn't you
          be destroying the world right about
          now? Pulling the sword out of Al
          Franken, or whatever he's called?

                                                         CONTINUED

36 CONTINUED: 36

                    ANGEL
          There's time enough. I wanted to say
          goodbye first. You are the one thing
          in this dimension I will miss.

                    BUFFY
                (suppressing emotion)
          This is a beautiful moment we're
          having here. Can we just fight,
          please?

                    ANGEL
                (hurt)
          I didn't come here to fight!

                    BUFFY
          No?

                    ANGEL
          Gosh, I was hoping we could get back
          together! What do you think, do we
          have a shot?

She glares at him.

                    ANGEL (cont'd)
          All right, we'll fight.

He lunges at her.

37 INT. LIBRARY - CONTINUOUS - NIGHT   37

Willow sits at the desk, the orb in front of her. Cordelia is waving a burning sage bush, not loving her task. Giles stands on Willow's other side, holding a volume. There are elaborate markings on the table and Willow has a painted mark on her forehead to match the Gypsy Woman's.

Xander stands up on the balcony, watching. Kendra guards the door.

                    GILES
                (Latin)
          Quod perditum est, invenietur.
          (What was lost, shall be found.)

                    WILLOW
          Not dead, nor not of the living.
          Spirits of the interregnum, I call.

38 EXT. GRAVEYARD - CONTINUOUS - NIGHT   38

Buffy and Angel spar, Buffy still holding back. Buffy is thrown to the ground.

> BUFFY
> (quietly)
> Come on, Willow...

39 INT. LIBRARY - CONTINUOUS - NIGHT   39

> WILLOW
> Let him know the pain of humanity, gods -- reach your wizened hands to me, give me the soul of --

ANGLE: XANDER

As two vamps burst in behind him. He turns to fight --

> XANDER
> Look out!

ANGLE: KENDRA

as she turns, two more burst in behind her.

ANGLE: XANDER

as he whips out a stake, makes for Vamp 1 as Vamp 2 comes down toward the ritual.

Kendra punches Vamp 3, sends him into the wall. Vamp 4 passes her.

As Vamps 2 and 4 converge in the middle, Cordy and Willow make for the stacks. Giles faces the vamps and they handily knock him down and out.

Vamp 1 grabs Xander's wrist, bends it. We hear it <u>snap</u> and Xander's eyes go wide.

Kendra spars with Vamp 3, knocking him out and going for Vamp 4, who stands over Giles.

Vamp 2 leads onto the table, over the railing and slams into a bookcase, knocking it over on Willow. She falls very hard, instantly unconscious.

Xander falls to his knees, the stake dropping. Cordy tries to get out behind Vamp 1. He turns to get her and Xander rises, throws him into Vamp 2.

CONTINUED

BUFFY THE VAMPIRE SLAYER "Season Finale, Part One" (WHITE) 3/6/98   50.

39   CONTINUED: 39

> XANDER (cont'd)
> Go!

Cordy races out as Xander picks up the stake in his good hand.

ANGLE: THE DOOR

Drusilla wafts in, eyes alight.

ANGLE: KENDRA

throws Vamp 4 through the window to Giles' office as Vamp 3 hits her from behind.

40   EXT. GRAVEYARD - CONTINUOUS - NIGHT   40

A quick exchange of blows.

> ANGEL
> Is it me, or is your heart not in this?

He throws her back.

> ANGEL (cont'd)
> Maybe I'll just go home. Destroy the world... sulk...

Buffy pulls out her stake.

> BUFFY
> I think Mister Pointy is gonna have something to say about that.

Angel hesitates.

> BUFFY (cont'd)
> Come on. Let's finish it. You and me.

Angel starts to laugh.

> ANGEL
> You never learn, do you? Little miss ego. 'You and me.' This wasn't about <u>you</u>. This was never about you.

Her expression drains. She turns and bolts, Angel calling after her.

> ANGEL (cont'd)
> And you fall for it <u>every single time!</u>

BUFFY THE VAMPIRE SLAYER "Season Finale, Part One" (WHITE) 3/6/98 51.

41 INT. LIBRARY - CONTINUOUS - NIGHT   41

Vamp 1 knocks Xander unconscious, looks down at

ANGLE: KENDRA

who is fighting off the other vamps. She's getting tired.

                    DRUSILLA
   Enough.

The vamps back off. Kendra turns to face Dru. Dru drops her shawl, looking dreamily into the heavens.

Kendra lunges and Dru evades, slashes as Kendra with her fingernails. Draws blood.

42 EXT. STREET - CONTINUOUS - NIGHT   42

Buffy races full speed for the school.

43 INT. LIBRARY - CONTINUOUS - NIGHT   43

Kendra and Dru spar, Kendra getting in some good hits, Dru mostly weaving and giggling.

Finally Dru sees an opening and grabs Kendra's throat, pushes her against the wall. Kendra struggles, pulling at the arm.

CLOSE ON: DRUSILLA'S EYES

Boring into Kendra, hypnotizing her.

                    DRUSILLA
   Look at me, Dearie. Be in my eyes.
   Be in me.

CLOSE ON: KENDRA'S EYES

as the will goes out of them.

Dru steps back, letting go. Kendra stands still, swaying slightly.

44 EXT. STREET - NIGHT   44

Buffy runs.

BUFFY THE VAMPIRE SLAYER "Season Finale, Part One" (WHITE) 3/6/98   52.

45 INT. LIBRARY - CONTINUOUS - NIGHT   45

   Dru pauses -- then slashes her fingers across Kendra's
   throat. Kendra's eyes widen -- she grabs her throat and
   blood wells out between her fingers.

   She drops.

                     DRUSILLA
                  (to Kendra)
              Night night.
                  (to the vamps)
              Let's get what we came for, dears.

   Two of the vamps bend down and lift up Giles -- start
   dragging him out.

46 INT. HALL/LOUNGE - LATER (NIGHT)   46

   Buffy bursts into the lounge, running as fast as she can. As
   the camera follows her she goes into slow motion, all sound
   bleeding out of the sound track.

                     WHISTLER (V.O.)
              Bottom line is even if you see 'em
              coming, you're not ready for the big
              moments. No one asks for their life
              to change, not really. But it does.

   Buffy enters the --

47 INT. LIBRARY - CONTINUOUS - NIGHT   47

   Sees the carnage.

   She spots Kendra lying on the ground, goes to her, cradles
   her on her lap -- tries to stop the bleeding as Kendra dies
   right in front of her.

                     WHISTLER (V.O.)
              So, what, are we helpless? Puppets?
              No. The big moments are gonna come,
              can't help that. It's what you do
              afterwards that counts. That's when
              you find out who you are.

   ANGLE: BUFFY AND KENDRA

   We see them from behind, Buffy still holding Kendra's head in
   her lap, when a policeman's GUN comes into frame.

                     COP
              Freeze!!

                                                          CONTINUED

47   CONTINUED: 47

ANGLE: TWO COPS

are pointing their weapons, looking mighty tense.

Buffy whips her head around to see them.

                                                    BLACK OUT.

Over the title: TO BE CONTINUED:

                        WHISTLER (V.O.)
                You'll see what I mean.

                        END OF SHOW

Episode # 5V22
Story # E00137

BUFFY THE VAMPIRE SLAYER

"Becoming, Part Two"

Written and Directed By

Joss Whedon

SHOOTING SCRIPT

March 13, 1998 (WHITE)
March 18, 1998 (BLUE PAGES)

BUFFY THE VAMPIRE SLAYER "Becoming, Part Two" (BLUE) 3/18/98

BUFFY THE VAMPIRE SLAYER

"Becoming, Part Two"

CAST LIST

```
BUFFY SUMMERS......................... Sarah Michelle Gellar
XANDER HARRIS......................... Nicholas Brendon
RUPERT GILES.......................... Anthony S. Head
WILLOW ROSENBERG...................... Alyson Hannigan
CORDELIA CHASE........................ Charisma Carpenter
ANGEL................................. David Boreanaz

SPIKE................................. James Marsters
DRUSILLA.............................. Juliet Landau
JENNY CALENDAR........................ Robia La Morte
OZ.................................... Seth Green
JOYCE................................. Kristine Sutherland
PRINCIPAL SNYDER...................... Armin Shimerman
WHISTLER..............................*Max Perlich
FIRST COP.............................*Susan Leslie
SECOND COP............................
BEAT COP..............................*Jim Hardy
*DETECTIVE STEIN (POLICE OFFICER)......* James McDonald
```

BUFFY THE VAMPIRE SLAYER

"Becoming, Part Two"

<u>SET LIST</u>

<u>INTERIORS</u>

SUNNYDALE HIGH SCHOOL
    LIBRARY
    HALLWAY
HOSPITAL
    ROOM
    CORRIDOR
SPIKE AND DRU'S MANSION
    SIDE ROOM
BUFFY'S HOUSE
    FOYER
    KITCHEN
    LIVING ROOM
    UPSTAIRS HALL
    BUFFY'S ROOM
GILES' APARTMENT
SPIKE'S CAR
BUS

<u>EXTERIORS</u>

STREET
FRONT LAWN
SPIKE AND DRU'S GARDEN
OUTSIDE SPIKE AND DRU'S MANSION
MANSION GARAGE
BUFFY'S HOUSE
FRONT OF SCHOOL
EDGE OF TOWN

BUFFY THE VAMPIRE SLAYER

"Becoming, Part Two"

TEASER

1   INT. LIBRARY - NIGHT (SECONDS AFTER RECAP)   1

A SECOND COP joins the first, also draws his weapon.

> SECOND COP
> Back away from the girl! Put your
> hands up and back away slowly!

> BUFFY
> But, I didn't--

> SECOND COP
> Do it now!

She does, as the first cop moves to Kendra, checks her vitals.

> FIRST COP
> This one's dead.

> SECOND COP
> What about up there?

ANGLE: XANDER

is visible lying on the balcony

> BUFFY
> Xander!

She starts for him, breaking away from second cop, but First Cop grabs her, throws her back.

> FIRST COP
> Get her out of here!

> BUFFY
> (re: Xander)
> See if he's okay!

Second Cop takes her and roughly pushes her through the doors to

2   INT. HALL - CONTINUOUS - NIGHT   2

As they come out we see Snyder arriving with two OTHER COPS.

CONTINUED

2 CONTINUED: 2

                         SECOND COP
               You'd do well to keep your mouth
               shut, missy.

                         BUFFY
               I didn't do anything!

                         SNYDER
               Why do I find that so very hard to
               believe?

                         SECOND COP
                    (to the other cops)
               In there.
                    (as they go inside,
                     to Snyder)
               You know this girl?

                         SNYDER
               Buffy Summers. If there's trouble,
               she's behind it.

                         BUFFY
               You stupid little troll, you have no
               idea --

                         SNYDER
               Attitude problem. Serious.

                         BUFFY
               Please, see if the others are okay...

                         SECOND COP
               That's enough.

He spins around, takes out his cuffs.

                         SECOND COP (cont'd)
               You have the right to remain silent.
               Anything you say --

She rears back and Pruitts the son of a bitch into
unconsciousness. She takes off, Snyder shrinking against the
wall --

                         SNYDER
               I'm just a civil servant...

-- the other cops coming out, guns drawn --

ANGLE: BUFFY

runs through the double doors--

                                                         CONTINUED

BUFFY THE VAMPIRE SLAYER "Becoming, Part Two" (WHITE) 3/13/98   3.

2   CONTINUED: (2)   2

                    FIRST COP (O.S.)
              Stop!

ANGLE: THE FIRST COP

running after her, stopping, **firing** --

-- a bullet smashing the window in one of the doors, just missing Buffy as she takes off out of the building.

The cop speaks into his walkie as the other takes off after Buffy.

                    COP
              All units, we have a fugitive on foot
              at the high school, homicide suspect,
              female, blonde, approximately sixteen
              years old, suspect is very
              dangerous --

                                                        BLACK OUT.

                        END OF TEASER

BUFFY THE VAMPIRE SLAYER "Becoming, Part Two" (WHITE) 3/13/98 4.

ACT ONE

3   INT. HOSPITAL CORRDIOR - NIGHT   3

It is fairly busy as Buffy walks in, keeping her head down. She has on an overcoat and hat, nothing too obvious. She searches around a bit, looking from room to room.

A hand reaches out and grabs her.

She spins to see:

                    BUFFY
          Xander!

She hugs him, tightly. Lets go and looks at him.

                    BUFFY (cont'd)
          I didn't know if you were okay. The
          cops -

                    XANDER
          Yeah, I heard them chase you out. I
          was just coming out of it.

Shows a cast on his wrist.

                    XANDER (cont'd)
          Souvenir.

                    BUFFY
          Well, what about the others? Are
          they --

He grabs her in another embrace as two cops walk by. Lets go as they leave.

                    BUFFY (cont'd)
          Okay, that was about equal parts
          protecting me and copping a feel,
          right?

He doesn't smile. Dread suffuses her.

                    BUFFY (cont'd)
          What is it?

4   INT. HOSPITAL ROOM - A FEW MOMENTS LATER - NIGHT   4

Willow lies unconscious in bed, hooked up to machines. Buffy approaches, distraught -- Xander behind her.

                                                        CONTINUED

4 CONTINUED: 4

> XANDER
> The doctor said it was... head trauma... she could wake up any time, but the longer it takes... the less likely it is.

> BUFFY
> I shouldn't have let her try to do the curse. Angel must have known.

Buffy doesn't speak. She runs her hand along Willow's forehead. After a moment she looks around her.

> BUFFY (cont'd)
> Where are her folks?

> XANDER
> With relatives, in Phoenix. I called them. They're getting a plane back.

> BUFFY
> Does Oz know?

> XANDER
> Man, I didn't even think. I'll call him.

Cordelia enters, tentatively. Xander spots her.

> XANDER (cont'd)
> Hey!

He crosses to her with a big relieved hug and kiss.

> BUFFY
> You're not hurt?

> CORDELIA
> I ran. I think I made it through three counties before I realized no one was chasing me. Not real brave.

> BUFFY
> It was the right thing to do.

> XANDER
> Did Giles keep up with you?

She looks at the two of them.

> CORDELIA
> I didn't see Giles.

CONTINUED

BUFFY THE VAMPIRE SLAYER "Becoming, Part Two" (WHITE) 3/13/98

4 CONTINUED: (2) 4

                    BUFFY
                (to Xander)
    You mean he's not in here?

                    XANDER
    No.

Off Buffy's inevitable conclusion:

5 INT. MANSION - NIGHT 5

Giles is on the floor, just beginning to come to. He looks around, trying to focus.

Angel is lying on his stomach, face near Giles', smiling.

                    ANGEL
    Hi, Rupert.

Giles rears back into a sitting position, looking about him. He is still very groggy.

Spike is sitting behind Angel. Two VAMPS flank Giles, a bit behind him.

Angel stands, as Giles attempts to.

                  ANGEL (cont'd)
    I wasn't sure you were gonna wake up.
    You had me worried.

                  GILES
    What do you want?

                  ANGEL
    I want to torture you. I used to
    love it, and it's been a long time.
    I mean, the last time I tortured
    someone they didn't even **have** chain
    saws.

The two vamps move a step closer to Giles as he finally gets to his feet, eyes widening in fear. He looks to the side and his gaze locks on something at the other end of the room.

ANGLE: THE STATUE OF ACATHLA

Stands alone, several feet away.

CONTINUED

5   CONTINUED: 5

                    ANGEL (cont'd)
                  (turns to look)
            Oh, yeah, Acathla. He's an even
            harder guy to wake up than you are.
            I performed this ritual, said all the
            right phrases, blood on my hand...
            got nothing. Big donut hole for my
            troubles. I figure you know the
            ritual; you're pretty up on these
            things, you could probably tell me
            what I'm doing wrong. But honestly,
            I sort of hope you don't...
                  (turning back to
                  Giles)
            ...'cause I **really** wanna torture you.

Giles looks right at Angel, shitscared. Then he suddenly
SLAMS his elbow into one of the vamps faces, knocking him
back. The other vamp comes at him and Giles hurls him into
Angel, takes off for the door.

He makes it as far as the door and Drusilla steps in through
it, grabbing Giles by the throat. Easily walking him back as
he chokes.

She hands him back to the two vamps. Angel comes up to him,
smiling as ever.

                    ANGEL (cont'd)
            Okay. Where do we start? Ooh.
            Fingers.

6   INT. BUFFY'S FOYER - NIGHT   6

Joyce is there, talking to a police officer, DETECTIVE STEIN.   *
Another comes down from upstairs holding a picture of Buffy.

                    JOYCE
            There's been some terrible mistake.

                    DETECTIVE STEIN   *
            And you have no idea where your
            daughter is?

                    JOYCE
            No, I --

Detective Stein takes the picture, looks at it.   *

                    DETECTIVE STEIN   *
            Do you always let your daughter stay
            out this late?

                                                              CONTINUED

6   CONTINUED: 6

                  JOYCE
No. She goes out; I can't always keep track, but...
              (remembering)
She said she was going to her friend Willow's house. Maybe she slept over.

              DETECTIVE STEIN
Is that Willow Rosenberg?

                  JOYCE
Yes...

              DETECTIVE STEIN
              (to the other)
Second victim.

                  JOYCE
What...?

              DETECTIVE STEIN
Does your daughter have a history of violence, Ms Summers?

                  JOYCE
Well... she's had some fights, but...

              DETECTIVE STEIN
You call us, okay? If she decides to stop by. It'd be best if she just comes in.

They let themselves out.

7   INT. GILES' APARTMENT - NIGHT 7

The door is slightly ajar as Buffy enters, calling out:

                  BUFFY
Giles? Giles!

Whistler comes in from the bathroom.

                WHISTLER
I don't think he's here.

Buffy stops, eyeing him suspiciously.

                  BUFFY
Who are you?

CONTINUED

7 CONTINUED: 7

                WHISTLER
        Whistler.

                BUFFY
        What are you doing here?

                WHISTLER
        Waiting for you.

                BUFFY
        Why?

                WHISTLER
        'Cause I need a date for the prom.
        My mother says I may attend, but no
        fondling.

Buffy pushes him against the wall. Her gesture is casual, but he hits pretty hard.

                BUFFY
            (incredibly calm)
        I have lost friends tonight, and I
        may lose more. If you have
        information worth hearing then I am
        grateful for it. If you want to make
        jokes then I will pull out your
        ribcage and wear it as a hat.

                WHISTLER
        He**LO** to the imagery. Very nice.

He moves away from her, straightening his outfit.

                WHISTLER (cont'd)
        You know, it wasn't supposed to go
        down like this. Nobody saw you
        coming. I figured this for Angel's
        big day, but I thought he was here to
        stop Acathla, not bring him forth.
        But you two made with the smootchies
        and now he's a creep again.

She hates to hear that. It takes her down a peg.

                BUFFY
        We didn't know...

                WHISTLER
        Hey, not here to judge. Body like
        yours -- I'd pretty much give up my
        soul for a shot at that, too.
            (more)

                                                CONTINUED

7 CONTINUED: (2)   7

>   WHISTLER (cont'd)
>   But it took Angel off the roster.
>   Which puts you on the spot in a big
>   way. What are you gonna do? What
>   are you prepared to do?
>
>   BUFFY
>   Whatever I have to.
>
>   WHISTLER
>   Or maybe I should ask, what are you
>   prepared to give up?

She stares at him.

>   BUFFY
>   You don't have anything useful to
>   tell me, do you? What are you, some
>   immortal demon sent down to even the
>   score between good and evil?
>
>   WHISTLER
>   Wow. Good guess.
>
>   BUFFY
>   Why don't you try getting off your
>   immortal ass and **fighting** evil once
>   in a while? 'Cause I'm tired of
>   doing this by myself.
>
>   WHISTLER
>   (serious)
>   In the end, you're always by
>   yourself. You're all you got --
>   That's the point.
>
>   BUFFY
>   Spare me.

She walks out. He follows a bit, telling her:

>   WHISTLER
>   The sword isn't enough. You gotta be
>   ready.
>   (she's gone)
>   You gotta know how to use it!

He stops, unsatisfied with the conversation.

>   WHISTLER (cont'd)
>   Man, this is gonna be close...

                                                      CONTINUED

BUFFY THE VAMPIRE SLAYER "Becoming, Part Two" (WHITE) 3/13/98   11.

8   EXT. STREET - NIGHT   8

Buffy crosses a street, moving quickly and keeping to herself. Suddenly she is nailed by a pair of headlights, which go on accompanied by the flashing of police lights.

Before Buffy can react the cop is out of his car, gun drawn. He steps up, never taking his eyes off her.

                   BEAT COP
      Hold it! Right there. Hands above
      your head. Do it!

He starts moving forward -- then hears something, spins -- and is knocked so hard he flips over onto the hood of the squad car, unconscious.

Buffy stares into the glare of the headlights as a figure steps out.

                   SPIKE
      Hello, love.

                                  BLACK OUT.

                END OF ACT ONE

ACT TWO

9   EXT. STREET - NIGHT (SECONDS LATER)   9

Buffy lunges at Spike, starts pummeling him. He takes a
couple of hits then knocks her back with one. As she gets up
again, whipping out a stake:

                    SPIKE
          Will you hold on for a second?

She doesn't look like she's gonna. He backs off a couple of
paces, putting up his hands.

                    SPIKE (cont'd)
          Hey! White flag here! I quit!

                    BUFFY
          Let me clear this up for you. We're
          mortal enemies. We don't get "time-
          out"s.

                    SPIKE
          You wanna go around, pet, I'll have
          a gay old time of it. You wanna stop
          Angel, well, then, we gotta play it
          a bit differently.

                    BUFFY
          What are you talking about?

                    SPIKE
          I'm talking about your ex, love. I'm
          talking about putting him in the
          bloody ground.

A beat.

                    BUFFY
          This has got to be the lamest trick
          you guys have ever thought up.

                    SPIKE
          He's got your watcher. Right now
          he's probably torturing him.

That stops her.

                    BUFFY
          What do you want?

                                                      CONTINUED

9 CONTINUED: 9

>   SPIKE
>   I told you. I wanna stop Angel.
>   (smiles)
>   I wanna save the world.
>
>   BUFFY
>   Okay. You do remember that you're a
>   vampire, right?
>
>   SPIKE
>   We like to talk big, vampires do.
>   "I'm gonna destroy the world," --
>   just toughguy talk, strutting around
>   with your friends over a pint of
>   blood.

As he speaks, he sits on the hood of the car. Pulls a cig and a lighter from the unconscious cop's breast pocket, and lights himself a smoke.

>   SPIKE (cont'd)
>   Truth is, I like this world. You got
>   dog racing, Manchester United, "Love
>   Boat", and you got people. Billions
>   of people walking around like Happy
>   Meals with legs. It's all right
>   here. But then someone comes along
>   with a vision. With a real passion
>   for destruction. Angel could pull it
>   off. Goodbye Picadilly, farewell
>   Leicester bloody Square, you see what
>   I'm saying?
>
>   BUFFY
>   Uh, sort of?
>
>   SPIKE
>   Why don't you put that stake down?
>
>   BUFFY
>   'Cause of the whole 'not believing
>   you' issue. You might not be down
>   with Angel but why would you ever
>   come to me?

He doesn't really want to answer that, but he knows he has to. He grinds out his cig on the car.

>   SPIKE
>   I want Dru back. I want it like it
>   was, before he came back.
>   (disgusted)
>   The way she acts around him...

                                                    CONTINUED

9 CONTINUED: (2)   9

                    BUFFY
          Oh, you're pathetic!

Instinctively, he punches her in the face. She punches him
equally hard then continues talking as if neither of them had
moved.

                    BUFFY (cont'd)
          I've got friends in the hospital --
          people have died --

                    SPIKE
          I wasn't in on that raiding party --

                    BUFFY
               (not stopping)
          -- and I may lose more of them, the
          whole world could be sucked into Hell
          and you need my help 'cause your
          girlfriend's a big ho? Let me take
          this opportunity to **not care.**

                    SPIKE
          I can't fight them both alone and
          neither can you!

She punches him again. But it seems to be her final
outburst. She comes down a bit, glaring at him.

                    BUFFY
          You're a killer.

                    SPIKE
          And I'm all you got.

A beat, and she puts her stake away.

                    BUFFY
          All right. Talk.

The cop on the hood of the car groans. Spike turns to him.

                    SPIKE
          Let me just kill this guy --

Buffy clears her throat. Spike turns back.

                    SPIKE (cont'd)
          Oh. Right.

                    BUFFY
          Come on. Let's get inside.

                                                          CONTINUED

BUFFY THE VAMPIRE SLAYER "Becoming, Part Two" (WHITE) 3/13/98   15.

9   CONTINUED: (3)   9

They take off for her house.

10   INT. HOSPITAL ROOM - NIGHT   10

Willow still lies unconscious. Xander sits by her bed, Cordelia in a chair nearby. She gets up, crosses to him.

     CORDELIA
 She's gonna be okay.

     XANDER
 Yeah...

     CORDELIA
 Do you want some coffee?

     XANDER
 I don't want to leave, she might --

     CORDELIA
 I'll get it.

     XANDER
 Thanks.

She goes. Xander turns back to Willow, holds her hand.

     XANDER (cont'd)
 Come on, Will...
    (he takes a moment,
    continues:)
 Look, you don't have a choice here.
 You gotta wake up. I need you, Will.
 How am I gonna pass trig? Who am I
 gonna call every night to talk about
 what we did all day? You're my best
 friend, you're always...

He leans in close.

     XANDER (cont'd)
 I love you.

ANGLE: HER HAND

squeezes his.

He looks at it, at her, as her head moves slightly. Eyes flutter. He leans in, with feverish hope --

     XANDER (cont'd)
 Willow?

             CONTINUED

10 CONTINUED: 10

                    WILLOW
               Oz...?

Xander takes a hit for a moment, then forgets about himself.
She's awake.

                    WILLOW (cont'd)
               Oz...?

                    OZ (O.S.)
               I'm here.

He is just entering the room. Xander stands, makes way for
Oz to come to the bed.

                    XANDER
               She's just waking up...

                    OZ
                    (to Willow)
               Hey, baby...

                    WILLOW
               Hi...
                    (sees Xander)
               Hi Xander...

                    XANDER
               Hi.
                    (to Oz)
               I'm gonna get a doctor.

He goes.

                    OZ
                    (to Willow)
               How do you feel?

                    WILLOW
                    (very weakly)
               My head feels big. Is it big?

                    OZ
               No, it's head-sized.

He kisses her on her headsized head.

                    WILLOW
               Is everybody else okay?

11 INT. MANSION SIDE ROOM - NIGHT   11

A small, bare room. Giles is tied to a chair, his jacket and
tie off and his sleeves rolled up. Blood has run down his
forehead and out of his nose (a tasteful amount) and one of
his hands is bloody and crooked from creative finger breaking.

Angel paces in front of him, having fun.

                    ANGEL
            Rupert, buddy, I'm here to tell you
            I'm impressed. How're you holding up?

                    GILES
            Never... better...

                    ANGEL
            Glad to hear it.

He squats down in front of Giles. We see only to their
shoulders as Angel reaches out.

                    ANGEL (cont'd)
            Now. Tell me when it hurts.

It's not clear what he does, but Giles goes white with pain.

12 EXT. BUFFY'S FRONT LAWN - NIGHT   12

Buffy and Spike make their way toward the house. Joyce pulls
up in her car.

                    JOYCE
            Buffy!

                    BUFFY
            Mom...

Joyce jumps out, good 'n' frantic.

                    JOYCE
            Buffy where have you been? Are you
            okay? The police were here. Are you
            okay? I went looking for you.

                    BUFFY
            Mom, let's go inside --

                    JOYCE
            Who is this man?
                (to Spike)
            Who are you?
                (to Buffy)
            Are you okay?

                                                         CONTINUED

12 CONTINUED: 12

                        BUFFY
                  MOM.

Joyce stops.

                        BUFFY (cont'd)
                  I'm okay. I was... busy... doing
                  something. And this is Spike, and he
                  was doing it too.

                        JOYCE
                  Doing what? Buffy, terrible things
                  have happened. What were you doing?

                        SPIKE
                  What, your mum doesn't know?

Buffy glares at him.

                        JOYCE
                  Know what?

                        BUFFY
                  That, uh, that, uh, I'm in a rock
                  band.

She gets similar looks from both Joyce and Spike.

                        BUFFY (cont'd)
                  Yes, a rock band, with Spike here...

                        SPIKE
                          (helping)
                  Right, she plays the... triangle --

                        BUFFY
                  -- drums --

                        SPIKE
                  Drums, yeah, she's hell on the old
                  skins, you know.

                        JOYCE
                  And what do you do?

                        SPIKE
                  Well, I sing.

                        BUFFY
                  Why don't we go inside now and talk
                  about it.

                                                              CONTINUED

12 CONTINUED: (2)   12

Buffy and Spike start inside. Joyce takes a moment, then starts to follow.

                   JOYCE
   Well, I'm not sure how I feel about
   this...

Buffy is almost at the porch --

                   BUFFY
   (to Spike)
   You think she's buying it?

-- when a VAMPIRE leaps from the bushes. It's one of Angel's henchmen, and he blows past the two of them --

-- right into Joyce. She gets a good look at his face and she yelps with fear. He roars.

Buffy grabs him before he can untangle himself from Joyce. She hurls him toward Spike, who decks him solidly, knocks him back to Buffy who kicks him, whips out a stake and dusts him.

Joyce is completely wide eyed.

Spike goes up to Buffy, casually looking at the spot where the vampire was.

                   SPIKE
   One of Angel's boys.

                   BUFFY
   Must have been watching me. Or you.

                   SPIKE
   He won't get the chance to tattle on
   us now.

                   JOYCE
   Buffy... what's going on?

Buffy goes to her mom, takes a deep breath.

                   BUFFY
   Mom... I'm a vampire slayer.

Off Joyce's reaction --

                                   BLACK OUT.

                  END OF ACT TWO

BUFFY THE VAMPIRE SLAYER "Becoming, Part Two" (WHITE) 3/13/98   20.

ACT THREE

13   INT. HOSPITAL ROOM - NIGHT   13

Willow is on the phone with Buffy.

                WILLOW
I'm okay, Buffy, really. I mean, don't feel good, but I'm awake and I know my name and who's president and how many fingers so they don't think my brain got mushed at all.

                            INTERCUT WITH:

14   INT. BUFFY'S KITCHEN/HOSPITAL ROOM - CONTINUOUS - NIGHT   14

Buffy is alone in the kitchen.

                BUFFY
Thank God... I'm sorry I can't be there.

                WILLOW
I know. I'm' sorry I didn't get to cure Angel.

                BUFFY
Don't be. I just think it wasn't meant to happen. I know I'm never gonna get Angel back the way he was and, you know, it makes it easier.

                WILLOW
I guess... Any luck finding Giles?

                BUFFY
Yes. I got a lucky break.

                WILLOW
What?

                BUFFY
You wouldn't believe me if I told you.

15   INT. BUFFY'S LIVING ROOM - CONTINUOUS - NIGHT   15

Joyce sits in the living room with Spike. They both are silent and uncomfortable, like it's Sunday and he's come a 'courtin'. Joyce has a glass of bourbon in her hands, which shakes only slightly.

BUFFY THE VAMPIRE SLAYER "Becoming, Part Two" (WHITE) 3/13/98   21.

16 INT. BUFFY'S KITCHEN/HOSPITAL ROOM - CONTINUOUS - NIGHT   16

(still INTERCUT with the hospital room, as Xander takes the phone)

BUFFY
Xander! Angel and the others are holed up outside town. You know that funky looking mansion you showed me one time?

XANDER
On Crawford Street. Sure. That makes sense. What's the drill?

BUFFY
I'm gonna hit the place come daybreak. I just need to get something first.

A17 INT. HOSPITAL ROOM/BUFFY'S KITCHEN - CONTINUOUS - NIGHT A17 *

XANDER
You'll need backup.

BUFFY
No. You stay there. I'm covered.

XANDER
Do you —

He pitches his voice low so the others won't hear —

XANDER (cont'd)
-- do you think Giles is still alive?

BUFFY
I think so. I just wish he was here to tell me what to do.

17 INT. BUFFY'S LIVING ROOM - CONTINUOUS - NIGHT   17

Another awkward beat. Joyce is pretty much just shell-shocked into politeness. After a bit:

JOYCE
Um, have we met?

SPIKE
You hit me with an axe one time.
        (imitating her)
"Get the Hell away from my daughter!"...

CONTINUED

BUFFY THE VAMPIRE SLAYER "Becoming, Part Two" (WHITE) 3/13/98   22*

17   CONTINUED: 17

                    JOYCE
          Oh. So... do you live here in town?

Before Spike can even reply to this inane comment, Buffy
enters. He and Joyce rise.

                    JOYCE (cont'd)
          Is Willow all right?

                    BUFFY
          She's fine.
               (to Spike)
          Talk to me. What's the deal?

                    SPIKE
          Simple. I help you kill Angel, you
          let me and Dru skip town.

                    JOYCE
          Angel? Your boyfriend?

                    BUFFY
          Forget about Drusilla. She doesn't
          walk.

                    SPIKE
          There's no deal without Dru!

                    BUFFY
          She killed Kendra.

                    SPIKE
               (genuinely proud)
          Dru bagged a slayer? She didn't tell
          me! Good for her!
               (off Buffy's look)
          Well, not from your perspective, I
          suppose...

                    BUFFY
          I can't beleive I invited you in my
          house.

                    JOYCE
               (to Buffy)
          So you didn't kill that girl?

                    BUFFY
          Of course not!

                    JOYCE
          Did she explode like those men
          outside?

                                              CONTINUED

17 CONTINUED: (2)   17

                    BUFFY
          She was a slayer, Mom.

                    JOYCE
          Like what you are?

                    SPIKE
               (to Buffy)
          Look, this deal works one way only.
          Full stop. Me and Dru for Angel.

                    JOYCE
          Honey, are you sure you're a slayer?

                    SPIKE
          I'll take her out of the country.
          You'll never hear from us again, I
          bloody well hope.

                    BUFFY
          All right. Get back to the mansion.
          Make sure Giles is all right.

                    JOYCE
          I mean, have you tried not being a
          slayer?

                    BUFFY
          Mom...
               (to Spike)
          Be ready to back me up when I make my
          move.

                    SPIKE
          Right.

                    BUFFY
          If Giles dies, **she** dies.

He glares at her, then exits.

                    JOYCE
          It's 'cause you didn't have a strong
          father figure. Isn't it.

                    BUFFY
          It's just fate, mom. I'm the Slayer.
          Accept it.

                    JOYCE
          We should call the police.

                                                          CONTINUED

17 CONTINUED: (3)   17

                    BUFFY
          We're not calling the police.

                    JOYCE
          Well, now that we know you're
          innocent...

                    BUFFY
          What, did you think I was guilty?
          Feeling the love in **this** room, jeez.

                    JOYCE
          I didn't think that... I just, now we
          have proof.

                    BUFFY
          We have my word, Mom. Not proof.

     Joyce crosses into -

18 INT. BUFFY'S KITCHEN - CONTINUOUS - NIGHT   18

     -- Buffy following.

                    JOYCE
          I'm sure they'll understand -

                    BUFFY
          You get them involved, you'll get
          them killed.

                    JOYCE
          You wouldn't hurt them, honey...

                    BUFFY
          Mom, I'm a slayer, not a postal
          worker. The cops just can't handle
          demons. I have to do it.

                    JOYCE
          Do what?

                    BUFFY
          I'm gonna need Kendra's sword.

                    JOYCE
          Sword? Buffy, what's happening?

                    BUFFY
                (impatiently)
          Just have another drink, okay?

                                                                CONTINUED

18 CONTINUED: 18

      JOYCE
  Don't you talk to me like that!

She hurls her glass to the floor, shattering it.

      JOYCE (cont'd)
  You can't just drop something like
  this on me and pretend it's nothing!

      BUFFY
  I'm sorry, I don't have time -

      JOYCE
  No! I'm tired of "I don't have time"
  and "You wouldn't understand." I am
  your mother and you are going to make
  time to explain yourself.

Buffy is a little cowed, though she still carries her impatient undertone.

      BUFFY
  I told you. I'm a vampire slayer.

      JOYCE
  Well, I don't accept that!

      BUFFY
  Open your eyes, Mom! What do you
  think has been going on for the last
  two years? The fights, the weird
  occurrences -- how many times have
  you washed blood out of my clothes,
  you still haven't figured it out?

      JOYCE
  Well, it stops now.

      BUFFY
  It doesn't stop. Do you think I
  chose to be like this? Do you know
  how lonely it is? How dangerous? I
  would love to be upstairs watching TV
  or gossiping about boys or god, even
  studying. But I have to save the
  world. Again.

      JOYCE
  No. This is insane. You need help.

      BUFFY
  I'm not crazy, Mom! What I need is
  for you to chill. I'll be back.

CONTINUED

18 CONTINUED: (2)   18

                         JOYCE
               I'm not letting you out of this house.

                         BUFFY
               You can't stop me.

She tries to leave and Joyce grabs her arm - Buffy flings her
hand off -- Joyce tries to grab her again and Buffy pushes
her hard against the wall. Goes to the door.

                         JOYCE
               You walk out of this house, don't
               even think about coming back.

A beat. Buffy leaves.

19 INT. HOSPITAL ROOM - NIGHT   19

A NURSE is just leaving, the kids waiting for her to go so
they can talk freely.

                         CORDELIA
               So Buffy's going for the big
               showdown, huh? I wish we could help.
               You know, without dying...

                         XANDER
               I don't see how.

                         WILLOW
               I want to try again.

                         OZ
               Try what?

                         WILLOW
               The curse. We never got to finish
               it. Maybe we **can** restore Angel's
               soul.

                         XANDER
               I don't like it. You're talking
               about messing with powerful magic,
               and you're weak.

                         WILLOW
               I'm okay.

                         XANDER
               You don't look okay. Does she?

                                                              CONTINUED

19 CONTINUED: 19

                    CORDELIA
          Listen to him. The hair is **so** flat,
          and, do you even **use** base?

                    XANDER
          Try to stay on topic here, honey.

                    CORDELIA
          What?

                    WILLOW
          There's no use arguing with me. Do
          you see my resolve face? You've seen
          it before and you know what it means.
                    (to Cordy)
          Just help me cast the spell and you
          can give me a complete makeover.

                    CORDELIA
          You're not just saying that?

                    WILLOW
          We can help Buffy -- if we turn Angel
          back soon enough, we can stop him
          from ever awakening Acathla.

                    OZ
          I pretty much missed out on some
          stuff, didn't I? 'Cause this is all
          making the kind of sense that's not.

                    WILLOW
          Go with Cordy to the library and get
          my things. She'll fill you in.

                    OZ
          Sure. I'll drive.

He and Cordy exit.

                    WILLOW
          Xander, you go to Buffy. Tell her
          what we're doing. Maybe she can
          stall.

                    XANDER
          But --

                    WILLOW
          Resolve face.

He's beat.

                                                        CONTINUED

19 CONTINUED: (2)   19

                    XANDER
              Be careful.

He exits.

20 INT. MANSION SIDE ROOM - DAYBREAK   20

Not that we can tell in this dark room. Giles is still tied
to the chair, looking even worse. Angel leans over from
behind him.

                    ANGEL
              You know I can stop the pain. You've
              been very brave, but it's over.
              You've given enough now let me make
              it stop.

                    GILES
              Please...

                    ANGEL
              Tell me what I need to know.

Giles looks at him, a broken man.

                    GILES
              To be worthy... you must perform the
              ritual... in a tutu.

Angel stares at him in mounting fury. Giles musters what he
can of a smile.

                    GILES (cont'd)
              Pillock.

Angel stands up abruptly.

                    ANGEL
              All right, that's it. Someone get
              the chain saw.

                    SPIKE
              Now now...

He rolls in, eyeing Angel.

                    SPIKE (cont'd)
              Don't let's lose our temper.

                    ANGEL
              Keep out of it, Sit'n'Spin.

                                                        CONTINUED

20 CONTINUED: 20

                    SPIKE
          You cut him up, you'll never get your
          answers.

                    ANGEL
                  (suspiciously)
          Exactly when did you become so level-
          headed?

                    SPIKE
          Right about the time you became so
          pig-headed. You have your way with
          him, you'll never get to destroy the
          world. And I don't fancy spending
          the next month trying to get
          librarian out of the carpet. There
          are other ways.

                    ANGEL
          Enlighten me.

                    SPIKE
                  (calls out)
          Drusilla... sweetheart...

She enters the room, all smiles.

                    SPIKE (cont'd)
          Do you want to play a game?

21 INT. LIBRARY - NIGHT   21

Buffy pushes away the police tape, enters the library. It's
as she left it, sans people. She crosses over to Kendra's
bag, picking it up off the floor.

She puts it on the table, opens it.

                    SNYDER
          You do know this is a crime scene,
          don't you?

He is standing at the doorway, smiling smugly.

                    SNYDER (cont'd)
          But then, you're a criminal, so that
          pretty much works out.

                    BUFFY
          You know I didn't do it. The police
          will figure it out.

                                                               CONTINUED

BUFFY THE VAMPIRE SLAYER "Becoming, Part Two" (BLUE) 3/18/98   30.

21 CONTINUED: 21

                    SNYDER
          In case you didn't notice, the police
          in Sunnydale are deeply stupid. It
          doesn't matter anyway. Whatever they
          find, you've proved too much of a
          liability for this school.

He steps up, breathing in the fresh air of a great morning.

                    SNYDER (cont'd)
          These are the moments you want to
          savor. You wish time would stop so
          you can live them over and over
          again. You're expelled.

Buffy lifts the sword out of the bag, looking at it. Snyder stops wanting to live this over and over.

Buffy starts towards him.

                    BUFFY
          You never ever got a single date when
          you were in high school, did you?

                    SNYDER
                (it's true)
          Your point being...

She passes him without comment, exits. After a moment, he pulls out his cell phone, speed-dials.

                    SNYDER (cont'd)
          It's Snyder. Tell the Mayor I have
          good news.

22 INT. MANSION SIDE ROOM - NIGHT   22

Giles and Drusilla are alone. He is barely conscious. She finishes cleaning the blood off his face. Smiles at him.

                    DRUSILLA
          Is that better? My poor boy...

She runs her hand through his hair, closes her eyes.

                    DRUSILLA (cont'd)
          Let's see what's inside.

She clutches his head. After a bit, something runs through her body.

                                                       CONTINUED

22 CONTINUED: 22

>   DRUSILLA (cont'd)
>   Of course...

She lifts his chin up so he can look her straight in the eyes.

>   DRUSILLA (cont'd)
>   Look at me... be in me...

She puts her hand over his eyes, shutting them.

>   DRUSILLA (cont'd)
>   See with your heart.

ANGLE: GILES' POV

As the hand is removed from his eyes, we see that it is JENNY CALENDAR that he sees.

>   GILES
>   Jenny...
>
>   JENNY
>   Rupert.
>
>   GILES
>   Oh, God, Jenny, I thought I'd lost
>   you...
>
>   JENNY
>   Shhh... I'll never leave you.

She holds him a moment. Moves then to untie him.

>   GILES
>   We have to get out of here...
>
>   JENNY
>   Slowly. You're weak...

He is freed, and puts his hand to her face.

>   GILES
>   It can't be you...
>
>   JENNY
>   Did you tell Angel? About the ritual?
>
>   GILES
>   No... but we have to get him away
>   from Acathla.
>
>   JENNY
>   Why? Is he close to figuring it out?

                                                                   CONTINUED

22 CONTINUED: (2)   22

                         GILES
                    Later...

He tries to rise but can't.

                         JENNY
                    Rest. Tell me what to do...

There seems to be hesitation is his eyes. She comes in close
to him, passion rising in her. Touching him.

                         JENNY (cont'd)
                    It's all right... We'll be
                    together... finally... we'll have
                    everything we never got to have...
                    never got to feel... just tell me
                    what to do.

                         GILES
                    Get Angel away from... Acathla...

                         JENNY
                    Angel himself? He's the key...

                         GILES
                    His blood. He must not...

                         JENNY
                    Shhh...

She stops his mouth with a kiss.

We're close on Giles kissing her -- pull back and around to
see it's Drusilla he's kissing, and that Spike and Angel are   *
at the doorway. They turn to each other, Angel gleeful.

                         ANGEL
                    The blood. Of course. The blood on
                    my hands must be my own. I am the
                    key that will open the door. My
                    blood. My life.
                         (suddenly matter of
                          fact)
                    Okay, kill him.

                         SPIKE
                    What if he's lying?

                         ANGEL
                    Yeah, good point. All right, don't
                    kill him.
                         (more)

                                                          CONTINUED

BUFFY THE VAMPIRE SLAYER "Becoming, Part Two" (WHITE) 3/13/98   33.

22 CONTINUED: (3)   22

                    ANGEL (cont'd)
               You know, I like having you watch my
               back, kind of like old times...

     As he speaks, they look over at the other two (now out of
     frame).

                    SPIKE
               Uh, Drusilla...

                    ANGEL
               Honey...

     ANGLE: DRUSILLA

     Is still hungrily making out with Giles.

                    SPIKE
               We are finished here, ducks...

     She pulls away from Giles, looking about her with sheepish
     pleasure.

                    DRUSILLA
               Sorry... I was in the moment.

     Giles stares at them, his expression draining as he realizes
     what's happened.

23   INT. GILES' APARTMENT - JUST BEFORE MORNING   23

     Buffy re-enters. The door is still open and Whistler is
     going through Giles' fridge.

                    BUFFY
               What did you mean, "the sword isn't
               enough."

                    WHISTLER
               You know, raiding an englishman's
               fridge is like dating a nun. You're
               never gonna get the good stuff.

                    BUFFY
               Tell me how to use it.

     He pulls out a bottle of Woodpecker cider, opens it. Comes
     into the living room as he replies.

                                                        CONTINUED

23 CONTINUED: 23

> **WHISTLER**
> Angel's the key. His blood will open the door to Hell. Acathla opens his big mouth, creates the vortex, then only Angel's blood'll close it. One blow. Send 'em both back to hell. But I strongly suggest you get there before that happens. The faster you kill Angel, the easier it'll be for you.
>
> **BUFFY**
> Don't worry about me.
>
> **WHISTLER**
> It's all on the line here, kid.
>
> **BUFFY**
> I can deal.
> (looks at the sword, at him)
> I got nothing left to lose.

She exits. He watches her go, genuine sadness suffusing his gaze.

> **WHISTLER**
> Wrong, kid. You got one more thing.

                                                          BLACK OUT.

                        END OF ACT THREE

BUFFY THE VAMPIRE SLAYER "Becoming, Part Two" (BLUE) 3/8/98   35.

ACT FOUR

24   EXT. OUTSIDE THE MANSION - MORNING   24

Yes, it's sunrise. Sue me.

Buffy makes her way down a green and tangled hill. She is stopped by a noise, finds Xander coming from a slightly different direction.

> BUFFY
> Xander!
>
> XANDER
> Cavalry's here. Cavalry's a frightened guy with a rock, but it's here.

He shows her his lame rock. She gives him a stake.

> XANDER (cont'd)
> This is better.

He loses the rock.

> BUFFY
> You're not here to fight. You get Giles out of there and run like Hell, understood? I can't protect you. I'm gonna be too busy killing.

Buffy unwraps the sword for herself, dropping the blanket.

> XANDER
> That's a new look for you.
>
> BUFFY
> It's a present for Angel. This ends it, Xander. I'm ready.

Xander looks down, trying to decide what to do.

> XANDER
> Willow... she said to tell you...
>
> BUFFY
> Tell me what?

He waits, decides.

> XANDER
> ...kick his ass.

CONTINUED

BUFFY THE VAMPIRE SLAYER "Becoming, Part Two" (BLUE) 3/18/98   36*.

24 CONTINUED: 24

                    BUFFY
           I'm gonna do a lot more than that.

    They head off for the mansion.

25 INT. MANSION - MORNING   25

    Sunlight is just beginning to peek in at the very tops of the
    window cracks. Angel stands in the same place he was for the
    ceremony last time. Dru and Spike behind him. Acathla still
    stands in front of the fireplace, two vamps flanking him.

                    ANGEL
                 (in Latin)
           Acathla. Mundatus sum. Pro te   *
           necavi. Sanguinem meum pro te   *
           effundam, quo me dignum esse   *
           demonstrem.   *
                 (Acathla. I have been cleansed. I   *
           have killed for you. I will bleed for
           you and prove myself worthy.)   *

26 INT. HOSPITAL ROOM - MORNING   26

    The door is shut. Cordelia has her herbs again, is not as
    put off by them -- she's all business. Willow is sitting up,
    has the orb in front of her. Oz has the book Giles was
    reading from.

                    WILLOW
           Are we ready?

                    CORDELIA
           Stinky herbs are go.

                    OZ
           Did I mention that I didn't take
           Latin?

                    WILLOW
           You don't have to understand it. you
           just have to say it. I hope.

                    OZ
           Right.
                 (reads slowly, in
                  latin)
           Quod perditum est, invenietur.
           (What was lost, shall be found.)

                                                         CONTINUED

26 CONTINUED: 26

                              WILLOW
                Not dead, nor not of the living...

27 INT. MANSION - MORNING   27

Drusilla steps up to Angel, hands him a knife. Spike sits a bit behind, watching with a cold eye.

Angel smiles at Dru, takes the knife and cuts his palm with it. Dru ripples with a little sensual trill at Angel's pain.

> ANGEL
> (in English)
> Now, Acathla, you **will** be free. And so will we all.

He takes a step forward -- and Buffy BURSTS IN through the doors from the garden.

The vamp nearest her makes a move, and she beheads him so quickly and tastefully the others barely have time to gape.

Buffy looks at Angel, sword at the ready.

> BUFFY
> Hello, lover.

> ANGEL
> I don't have time for you.

> BUFFY
> You don't have a lot of time **left**.

> ANGEL
> Coming on kind of strong, don't you think? You're playing some deep odds here -- do you really think you can take us all on?

> BUFFY
> No, I don't.

Spike rises behind Angel, hoisting a nasty looking iron poker. He SLAMS it into the back of Angel's head. Angel goes flying face first onto the ground as Spike moves forward, hits him again.

ANGLE: DRUSILLA

looks at Spike aghast.

Buffy makes for Angel -- and is hit from behind by Vamp Two. Her sword goes flying out of her hand and she stops to spar with the vamp.

ANGLE: SPIKE

is still wailing on Angel --

CONTINUED

BUFFY THE VAMPIRE SLAYER "Becoming, Part Two" (BLUE) 3/18/98   38.

27 CONTINUED: 27

>   SPIKE
>   Painful, isn't it?

-- when Dru tackles him from the side and they both go flying.

ANGLE: XANDER

during the melee, he sneaks in from the garden, moving quietly around the perimeter of the hall towards Giles' room.

ANGLE: BUFFY

spars with the vamp.

ANGLE: SPIKE AND DRU

come up facing each other. She's righteously pissed.

>   SPIKE (cont'd)
>   I don't want to hurt you, baby...

She grabs his throat and slams him against the wall. Instinctively, he knocks her arm away and deckS her as hard as he can.

>   SPIKE (cont'd)
>   Doesn't mean I won't...

28 INT. MANSION SIDE ROOM - CONTINUOUS - MORNING   28 *

Xander comes in, finds Giles tied to the chair, goes to him.

>   XANDER
>   Giles. Giles!
>
>   GILES
>   Xander?
>
>   XANDER
>   Can you walk?
>
>   GILES
>   You're not real...
>
>   XANDER
>   I am too real! Let's go!
>
>   GILES
>   It's a trick! They get inside my
>   head, make me see what I want.

                                                          CONTINUED

28 CONTINUED: 28

                      XANDER
      Then why would they make you see **me**?

Beat.

                      GILES
      Right. Let's go.

They start out.

29 INT. MANSION - CONTINUOUS - MORNING 29

Xander helps Giles toward the exit. They make it out to the garden and are gone.

ANGLE: DRUSILLA

throws Spike to the ground, hissing with anger.

ANGLE: ANGEL

Pulls himself painfully up and stumbles toward Acathla.

ANGLE: BUFFY

Pulls out a stake and kills the vamp.

She turns to look for Angel, sees:

ANGLE: ANGEL

reaches the statue.

Buffy dives for her sword, grabs it and heads for Angel.

Angel grabs the sword handle.

As before, light fills the room, stopping Buffy in her tracks as Angel is momentarily transported with electric bliss.

He pulls the sword free.

ANGLE: DRUSILLA

stops to look, gleeful.

                      DRUSILLA
      Oooh, here it comes...

Spike rises up behind her and gets her in a chokehold.

ANGLE BUFFY AND ANGEL

                                              CONTINUED

29 CONTINUED: 29

As they square off, swords at the ready. Like Dru said: here it comes.

                    ANGEL
      You almost made it, Buf.

                    BUFFY
      It's not over yet.

                    ANGEL
      My boy Acathla's about to wake up.
      You're going to Hell.

                    BUFFY
      Save me a seat.

And she comes at him, fast, hard, and it's **swordfight time**. Their blades are a blur of metal as they work at each other, driving back, forward, circling each other...

Angel draws first blood, on Buffy's arm.

30 INT. HOSPITAL ROOM - CONTINUOUS - MORNING   30

Willow continues the ritual.

                    WILLOW
      Gods, bind him, cast his heart from
      the demon... realm... return his...

She is breathing heavily, the words coming slowly, with difficulty. Perspiration beads her face.

                    WILLOW (cont'd)
      I call on... I...

                    OZ
      Willow?

                    CORDELIA
      Are you okay?

ANGLE: BIRDS EYE VIEW OF WILLOW

As her head snaps back, leaving her staring almost directly in camera, her whole body tensing --

-- and her head snaps back down, she starts to shake and she begins speaking the rest of the ritual rapidly, powerfully, **and in Rumanian**.

                                                      CONTINUED

BUFFY THE VAMPIRE SLAYER "Becoming, Part Two" (WHITE) 3/13/98   41.

30 30 CONTINUED: 30

                    WILLOW
          Te implor Doamne, nu ignora accasta
          rugaminte! Lasa orbita sa fie vasul
          care-i va transporta sufletul la el!
          (I call on you, Gods, do not ignore
          this supplication! Let the orb be
          the vessel to carry his soul to him!)

                    OZ
               (to Cordy)
          Is this a good thing?

                    CORDELIA
               (to Willow, not
                knowing what to say)
          Hey! Speak english!

                    WILLOW
          Este scris, aceasta putere este
          dreptul poporuil meu de a conduce...
          (It is written, this power is my
          people's right to wield...)

    ANGLE: THE ORB

    Begins to glow.

31 EXT. THE GARDEN - CONTINUOUS - MORNING   31

    For a moment it's quiet. The sun is high enough to hit half
    of the staircase, the rest is still dark.

    Buffy comes tumbling out, Angel behind her. He's definitely
    winning. He knocks the sword from her grasp, kicks her into
    a corner.

32 INT. MANSION - CONTINUOUS - MORNING   32

    ANGLE: ACATHLA

    The camera moves in at him as he begins to shake slightly,
    and we hear a humming sound.

    ANGLE: SPIKE AND DRU

    Dru is sinking into unconsciousness, Spike never loosening
    his grip on her neck. As she fades, he kisses her cheek.

                    SPIKE
          I wish there was another way...

                                                          CONTINUED

BUFFY THE VAMPIRE SLAYER "Becoming, Part Two" (WHITE) 3/13/98   42*.

32 CONTINUED: 32

He picks her up and starts for the exit near the doors to the garden. Pauses long enough to see:

ANGLE: THE GARDEN

As Angel approaches Buffy, sword in hand.

>   SPIKE (cont'd)
>   God, he's gonna kill her...

After a moment of intense worry, he shrugs, takes off.

33 EXT. GARDEN - CONTINUOUS - MORNING   33

Angel approaches Buffy. She tries to move from the corner, but he moves with her. She's boxed in.

He plays the sword near her face, loving this.

>   ANGEL
>   That's everything, huh? No weapons,
>   no friends. No hope. Take all that
>   away and what's left?

Buffy stares at him, his words hitting home. She looks exhausted, and terribly sad. She shuts her eyes.

He lunges, shooting his arm out, the sword straight at her face.

Without opening her eyes she slams her palms together over the blade, stopping it an inch from her face.

She opens her eyes.

>   BUFFY
>   Me.

She jerks the sword back, knocking the hilt into his face, kicking him solidly in the chest.

34 EXT. MANSION GARAGE - CONTINUOUS - MORNING   34

As Spike's car bursts out through the garage door, takes off down the road. The windows have all been blacked out except for enough space to see out of.

BUFFY THE VAMPIRE SLAYER "Becoming, Part Two" (BLUE) 3/18/98   43*.

35   INT. SPIKE'S CAR - CONTINUOUS - MORNING   35

    Dru is still passed out, sitting in the passenger seat.
    Spike drives with glum determination.

36   INT. MANSION - CONTINUOUS   36

    Angel flies in, lands hard -- gets up again and she is on
    him, sword in hand, pounding at him, driving him back until
    they are right in front of Acathla.

    She knocks his sword out of his hand -- cutting him on the   *
    hand. He stands before her, spent, beaten.   *

37   INT. HOSPITAL ROOM - CONTINUOUS - MORNING   37

    Willow is still rapt, calling out:

                    WILLOW
              Asa sa fie! Acum!
              (Let it be so! Now!)

    ANGLE: THE ORB

    Glows and disappears, just as it did before.

38   INT. MANSION - CONTINUOUS - MORNING   38

    Angel drops to his knees. Buffy swings her sword back, ready
    to cut off his head.

    Suddenly he cries out in pain, and she sees:

    CLOSE ON: HIS EYES

    They glow for a moment.

    He collapses to the floor. Buffy hesitates.

                    ANGEL
              Oh...

    He looks up.

                    ANGEL (cont'd)
              Buffy?

    He pulls himself up. She takes a step back, uncertain.

                                                        CONTINUED

38 CONTINUED: 38

>   ANGEL (cont'd)
>   Buffy, what's going on? I don't
>   remember.. where are we?

Her voice is very little when she speaks.

>   BUFFY
>   Angel?
>
>   ANGEL
>   (sees her cuts)
>   You're hurt!

He goes to her, takes her arm. Her swordarm hangs at her side, limp. He folds her into his arms.

>   ANGEL (cont'd)
>   God, I feel like I haven't seen you
>   in months... Buffy, everything's so
>   muddled...

ANGLE: BUFFY'S FACE

As he holds her. At first afraid, confused, but at the warmth of his touch, this overwhelming rush of his return, her eyes close and with her free arm she grips him to her.

>   ANGEL (cont'd)
>   Oh, Buffy...

She opens her eyes, longing and hope in them. Then they see it.

CLOSE ON ACATHLA

The demon opens his mouth. Wide. We hear a low rumble, growing louder as the vortex (not unlike that Sliders thing) begins to emanate from his mouth.

She grips Angel tighter, despair gutting her.

ANGLE: BUFFY AND ANGEL

Are framed in front of the growing vortex.

>   ANGEL (cont'd)
>   What's happening, Buffy?
>
>   BUFFY
>   Shhhhh... it doesn't matter.

She pulls away to look at him. Kisses him passionately.

                                                          CONTINUED

BUFFY THE VAMPIRE SLAYER "Becoming, Part Two" (WHITE) 3/13/98   45.

38 CONTINUED: (2)   38

                    BUFFY (cont'd)
              I love you.

                    ANGEL
              I love you...

                    BUFFY
              Close your eyes.

Serenely compliant, he closes them. She kisses him softly.

She steps back and **thrusts the sword through his chest**, directly into the chest of the demon.

There is an unearthly roar.

Angel's eyes open wide -- he looks down at himself impaled, at Buffy uncomprehendingly.

Buffy can't speak -- she tries not to cry as she takes another step back.

Angel reaches out to her -- and the vortex closes over him, sucks him into Hell. And is gone.

ANGLE: ACATHLA

His mouth closed once more.

ANGLE: BUFFY

Alone.

INCREDIBLY POIGNANT SARAH MCLACHLAN SONG BEGINS OVER:

39 EXT. BUFFY'S HOUSE - MORNING   39

Buffy walks slowly up to it, stops on the side walk. Looks at the house for a while.

40 INT. UPSTAIRS HALL - MORNING   40

Joyce comes upstairs in her dressing gown. She sees the door to Buffy's room open, starts in.

                    JOYCE
              Buffy?

41 INT. BUFFY'S ROOM - CONTINUOUS - MORNING   41

Joyce enters. The window is open, the curtains blowing in the breeze. Some of the drawers have been left open, clothes hanging out.

There is a note on the bed.

Joyce goes to it, picks it up. She reads it, and her eyes fill with tears.

42 EXT. FRONT OF SCHOOL - MORNING   42

Giles and Xander greet Oz, Cordelia and Willow. Oz pushes Willow in a wheelchair. Giles doesn't exactly look his best either.

                    GILES
                (to Willow)
        Are you sure you should be out of bed?

                    WILLOW
        Look who's talking...

                    CORDELIA
        Any word?

                    XANDER
        You guys didn't see her either.

                    WILLOW
        No.

                    OZ
        But we know the world didn't end.
        'Cause, check it out.

                    GILES
        We went back to the mansion. It's
        empty, and Acathla is dormant.

                    WILLOW
        I think the spell worked. I felt
        something go through me, it was
        powerful. Kind of scary.

                    CORDELIA
        Plus the orb did that cool glow thing.

                    XANDER
        Maybe it wasn't in time. If he did
        pull the sword out, and she had to
        kill him, maybe he was already dead
        when it happened.

                                              CONTINUED

42 CONTINUED: 42

                    OZ
          Then she'd want to be alone, I guess.

                    WILLOW
          Or maybe Angel was saved and they
          just want to be alone together.

                    GILES
          Perhaps.

                    CORDELIA
          Well, she's bound to show up sooner
          or later. We still have school.

                    WILLOW
          Yeah. She'll be here in a while.

ANGLE: BUFFY

is watching them from the far end of the big lawn triangle. She is dressed very plainly, for hard travelling. Has a bag over her shoulder.

As she sees them head inside, she starts walking in the other direction.

DISSOLVE TO:

43 ANGLE: THE EDGE OF TOWN, PASSING BY (INT. BUS - DAY)   43

Houses, fewer and fewer, as they whip by the window.

ANGLE: BUFFY

Seated on a bus, looking out the window as the light plays on her face.

44 EXT. EDGE OF TOWN - DAY   44

The bus races past camera and recedes in the distance, as the camera arms down, finally settling on a sign by the side of the road.

NOW LEAVING SUNNYDALE

COME BACK SOON

                                                      BLACK OUT.

                        END OF SHOW

"Well, we could grind our enemies into powder with a sledgehammer, but gosh, we did that last night."

—Xander

As long as there have been vampires, there has been the Slayer. One girl in all the world, to find them where they gather and to stop the spread of their evil and the swell of their numbers.

LOOK FOR A NEW TITLE EVERY MONTH!

Based on the hit TV series created by
Joss Whedon

Everyone's got his demons....

ANGEL™

If it takes an eternity, he will make amends.

Original stories based
on the TV show
Created by Joss Whedon
& David Greenwalt

Available from Simon Pulse
Published by Simon & Schuster

™ and © 2000 Twentieth Century Fox Film Corporation. All Rights Reserved.

2311-01

ROSWELL™

ALIENATION DOESN'T END WITH GRADUATION

Everything changed the day Liz Parker died. Max Evans healed her, revealing his alien identity. But Max wasn't the only "Czechoslovakian" to crash down in Roswell. Before long Liz, her best friend Maria, and her ex-boyfriend Kyle are drawn into Max, his sister Isabel, and their friend Michael's life-threatening destiny.

Now high school is over, and the group has decided to leave Roswell to turn that destiny around. The six friends know they have changed history by leaving their home.

What they don't know is what lies in store...

Look for a new title every other month from Simon Pulse—the only place for *all-new* Roswell adventures!

SIMON PULSE
Published by Simon & Schuster

. . . A GIRL BORN
WITHOUT THE FEAR GENE

FEARLESS™

A SERIES BY
FRANCINE PASCAL

PUBLISHED BY SIMON & SCHUSTER

AN AGELESS VENDETTA, AN ETERNAL LOVE, AND A DEADLY POWER...

"I'm living in a new town with a new family, and suddenly I'm discovering new powers, having new experiences, and meeting all sorts of new people. Including Jer. So why does it feel like I've known him forever? Even before I was born? It's almost like . . . magic."

WICKED

From best-selling author Nancy Holder comes a new series about star-crossed lovers from rival witch families.

Book One: WITCH

**Available October 2002
From Simon Pulse**

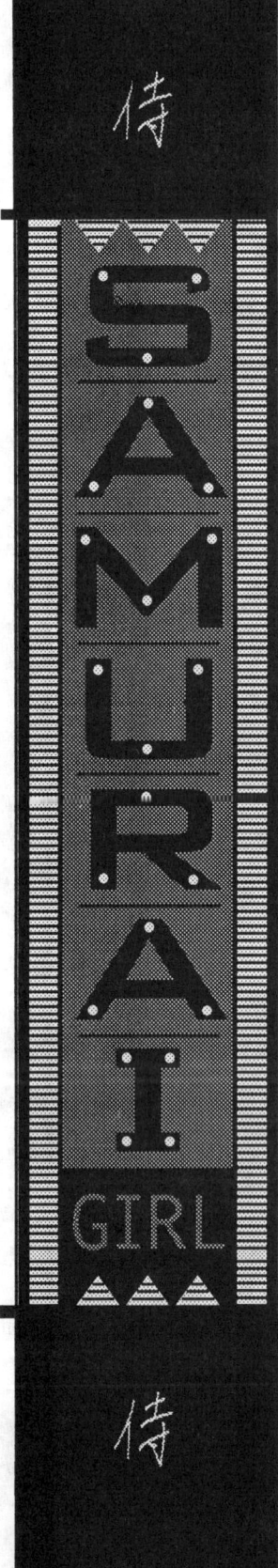

When I was six months old, I dropped from the sky—the lone survivor of a deadly Japanese plane crash. The newspapers named me Heaven. I was adopted by a wealthy family in Tokyo, pampered, and protected. For nineteen years, I thought I was lucky.
I'm learning how wrong I was.

I've lost the person I love most.
I've begun to uncover the truth about my family.
Now I'm being hunted. I must fight back, or die.
The old Heaven is gone.

I AM SAMURAI GIRL.

A new series from Simon Pulse

The Book of the Sword
The Book of the Shadow

Available in bookstores now